MW01252684

ary

# COMMODORE PERRY
## Opens Japan to Trade
## in World History

# Titles *in World History*

# COMMODORE PERRY
## Opens Japan to Trade
## in World History

Ann Graham Gaines

**Enslow Publishers, Inc.**

| | |
|---|---|
| 40 Industrial Road | PO Box 38 |
| Box 398 | Aldershot |
| Berkeley Heights, NJ 07922 | Hants GU12 6BP |
| USA | UK |

http://www.enslow.com

**Library of Congress Cataloging-in-Publication Data**

Gaines, Ann.
    Commodore Perry opens Japan to trade in world history / Ann Graham
Gaines.
        p. cm. — (In world history)
    Includes bibliographical references and index.
    Summary: Traces the efforts of Commodore Matthew Perry to use
force and diplomacy to end Japan's traditional isolationism and to begin
trade with the Asian nation.
    ISBN 0-7660-1462-2
    1. United States Naval Expedition to Japan, 1852–1854—Juvenile
literature. 2. United States—Foreign relations—Japan—Juvenile
literature. 3. Japan—Foreign relations—United States—Juvenile
literature. 4. Perry, Matthew Calbraith, 1794–1858—Juvenile literature.
[1. United States Naval Expedition to Japan, 1852–1854. 2. United
States—Foreign relations—Japan. 3. Japan—Foreign relations—United
States. 4. Perry, Matthew Calbraith, 1794–1858.] I. Title. II. Series.
DS881.8 .G35    2000
327.73052—dc21
                                  99-050739

**Illustration Credits:** Enslow Publishers, Inc., pp. 22, 43, 53, 63; Library
of Congress, pp. 9, 38, 51, 54, 58, 72, 73, 75, 83, 99, 104; Matthew Perry,
*Narrative of the Expedition of an American Squadron to the China Seas
and Japan* (New York: D. Appleton Co., 1856), p. 77; Reproduced from
the *Dictionary of American Portraits,* Published by Dover Publications,
Inc., in 1967, pp. 30, 35, 52; United States Naval Academy Museum,
p. 48; Watanabe Shujiro, *Abe Masahiro jiseki Nihon kaikoku kigen shi*
(Tokyo: Chosha, Meiji 43, 1910), p. 14.

**Cover Illustration:** Library of Congress (Matthew Perry portrait);
© Digital Vision Ltd. (Background).

# Contents

# Chapter 1

# The Black Ships Arrive

On the morning of July 8, 1853, four warships painted black, two paddle-wheeled steamships, and two sloops of war, together carrying 977 United States sailors, entered the fog-shrouded waters near the coast of the island nation of Japan. The U.S.S. *Mississippi* and the U.S.S. *Susquehanna* belched smoke and cinders into the sky from their coal-powered furnaces as they towed the U.S.S. *Saratoga* and the U.S.S. *Plymouth* behind them. Japanese sailors on board their own ships, called junks, saw the intruders through patches of fog. Quickly and quietly the Japanese turned their junks around to try to outrace the black ships and deliver the astounding news at home.

According to one early story that circulated among the Japanese, the foreign invaders were devils who had captured volcanoes and imprisoned them beneath the decks of their ships, using their force to move the ships through the water. The smoke and cinders flying into the sky from the hole in the smokestack proved it. In truth, of course, it was not a volcano that the engineers from the United States Navy had captured inside their ships, but it was a monster all the same— a mechanical monster that devoured tons of coal each day, one shovelful at a time, creating energy that pushed the ship through the water as fast as any wind.

These steamships were the technological marvel of the 1850s. They could go where they wanted whenever they pleased, and they carried new and deadly cannons, making them especially dangerous.

## The Guns

The cannons that the Japanese used at the time were the same kind used in Europe in the sixteenth century. They were made from cast iron and fired a solid iron ball through a barrel that had smooth sides. They were called smooth bore cannons. They had an effective range of little more than three hundred fifty yards. The steamships, on the other hand, carried an improved cannon that made Japanese opposition to the Americans out of the question.

In the early nineteenth century, engineering advances in the United States and France made it possible to make larger, heavier cannons that fired explosive shells. These shells were manufactured to be the right size for the barrels of the new guns. This made the new guns far more accurate. In addition, the new shells were hollow and filled with gunpowder.

*Steamships made the United States Navy far more dangerous than ever before. This is an artist's depiction of the trial run of the first steam-propelled warship in 1814.*

They exploded like bombs when they hit their target. These new naval guns were called Paixhan (pronounced "pay-on") guns. The barrels of these larger guns weighed as much as ten thousand pounds. These guns were accurate to two miles.[1] The *Mississippi* and the *Susquehanna* had been built with the support these guns needed so that they could be fired without tearing the ship apart. The *Mississippi* carried ten Paixhan guns. The *Susquehanna* had six.[2] The combination of steam power and the new guns made the ships almost invincible. These ships could remain out of the range of enemy guns while destroying any and all targets. These were the weapons of mass destruction in the 1850s.

## Commodore Matthew Calbraith Perry

The naval officer who commanded this mighty fleet was as imposing as the ships he commanded. Commodore Matthew Calbraith Perry had been in service almost since the United States Navy was created. He began his career in 1809 as a young apprentice aboard his older brother's armed schooner *Revenge*.[3] By 1851, he was a "crusty old salt" of fifty-six years, forty-one of which he had spent in the navy.

Commodore Perry seemed a stern and mysterious character to the men of the Black Fleet, the name given to the expedition because of the color of the ships. He was seldom seen. He left the day-to-day operations of the ships to their captains and other officers. He often worked alone at night in his cabin, preparing for his important mission to Japan. When he did emerge, everyone left him alone so he could think. When Perry appeared on the deck of the *Mississippi*, he would wear spotless white gloves. If his gloves showed any dirt after he inspected the ship, his crew members knew they had a big problem. The commodore, called "Old Matt," "Old Bruin," and "Big-whiskered Perry" behind his back by his men, had a reputation for strict discipline. Flogging had just recently been abolished by the navy as a punishment. Perry thought that was a shame. He believed that plenty of hard work, little time ashore, and a healthy dose of flogging for those who did not perform their duty were the best ways to maintain a happy, effective ship.

## The Fleet Arrives

Around ten in the morning, the fog started to lift. The sun shone through the haze above the hills and the beautiful snow-clad slopes rising in the distance some sixty miles away. The order "General Quarters," the call to prepare for battle, rang out aboard the ships of the Black Fleet. Everyone ran to his battle station, guns were loaded, and medical crews stood ready to tend the wounded.

At first, the small Japanese boats in the harbor ran away from the black ships. When the American intruders were seen simply ignoring the many small fishing boats in the channel, some approached for a closer look. At two in the afternoon, the black ships entered Tokyo Bay, a ten-mile-wide inlet at the end of which was the capital city of Japan—Tokyo, which was then called Edo. The black ships moved right into the heart of the country, the home of the powerful shogun, or prime minister.

William Heine, the twenty-five-year-old artist of Perry's expedition, was astonished by the beauty of the scene he saw. He wrote,

> Moderate elevations frame the bay in a hilly landscape; mountains rise higher at a distance. The hills sometimes end in bluffs [at the water's edge]: picturesque, lush with vegetation, and crowned by sublime and lovely pines. Elsewhere the hills expire into meadowed valleys and small flats. Towns and villages often occur there, as well as green handsome rice paddies wherever tillage is possible. . . . To heighten the charm, a haze cloaks the land in a delicate gray, softening and calming the impression. And, as foreground, the deep blue sea harmonizes beautifully.[4]

The ships moved to within a mile and a half of shore and anchored in battle formation with each ship's guns aimed to fire at the sparkling town of Uraga, a small fishing village at the mouth of Tokyo Bay. No European ship had ever before anchored in Tokyo Bay.

Once the ships had come to a stop in the water, the many small Japanese boats that were following behind came alongside. These brave sailors overcame their fears in order to see who these strangers were. American sailors on the decks of the black ships used long poles to push the small boats away.

Along the beach there was mass confusion. People were running in every direction. Fireworks exploded in the sky to warn others of the sudden appearance of the foreigners. Bells were rung. Women in the temples prayed for a divine wind, a *kamikaze*, to come and save them from the invaders.[5]

Not everyone in Japan was unprepared for the arrival of the Black Fleet. In 1852, the Dutch government informed the office of the shogun that an American naval officer, Matthew Calbraith Perry, would lead an expedition of four ships to Japan, seeking trade and a coaling station in the country. The shogun, Ieyoshi Tokugawa, was fifty-nine years old. He was the twelfth member of the Tokugawa family to serve as shogun since 1603. The news of Perry's expedition never reached him. He was sick and lived alone in his family castle in Tokyo. Because he was sick, he had given all the day-to-day powers of government to his assistant, Abe Masahiro, who received word of the Perry expedition. Japan also had an emperor, who was the symbolic head of the nation. It was the shogun who held real political power. However, Japanese officials felt it was important that the Americans never got to meet either the shogun or the emperor. They would deal only with lesser officials.

Abe Masahiro led a huge and efficient government to keep order in the country. More than seventeen thousand men worked at over two hundred jobs. These men produced nothing themselves. They were what is called a bureaucracy. They simply made sure

*Abe Masahiro (seen here) ran the Japanese government at the time of Commodore Perry's first visit, under the permission of the shogun, Ieyoshi Tokugawa.*

that everyone else worked for the benefit of the country as a whole. This governmental bureaucracy in Japan was called the *Bakufu*.

The news of the coming American expedition went directly from the Dutch community at Nagasaki through the different offices of the Bakufu to Abe Masahiro. He directed the several commanders of the military defenses of Tokyo to be ready. It would take time to prepare defenses and routes of evacuation for a population of well over a million people. Tokyo was perhaps the largest city on Earth at that time. Masahiro needed to give the military commanders time to prepare, even if the report ultimately turned out to be untrue. Earlier reports of approaching foreigners had turned out to be false. In 1838, the Dutch had sent word that the British were going to send an expedition to Japan, but nothing had come of it. When Abe Masahiro told the military commanders to prepare for Perry's expedition, many did not believe that this visit by foreigners would happen either. When Perry appeared with his Black Fleet, it truly was a surprise to many Japanese.

## First Confrontation

Kayama Eizaemon was a *yoriki*, a police magistrate and assistant to the city governor of Uraga. When Perry's fleet anchored less than a mile from his office, Kayama climbed aboard his official guard boat and went to meet Perry's ships. His small boat had a black tassel at the bow and a white flag with three horizontal black stripes to show it was the boat of a government official. The boat was rowed by several oarsmen who shouted out with each powerful stroke. The boat quickly reached the anchored *Susquehanna*.

When Kayama reached the American ships, he found Nakajima Saburonosuke, his fellow yoriki for Uraga, standing in another guard boat, holding up a sign with a message. It read, "Depart immediately and dare not anchor."[6] In poor Japanese, one of the American officers shouted that the Americans wanted to contact a high Japanese government official to whom they could deliver a letter from Millard Fillmore, the president of the United States.

The Japanese now faced an unwanted visit from a powerful foreign nation. Commodore Matthew Perry was determined to force Japan to open trade with the United States. And the Japanese would be powerless to stop him.

# Chapter 2

# Japan

Nineteenth-century Japan would seem to modern-day Americans a very strange place. It was a land of great cruelty and great beauty. Its people considered wearing the skins of animals barbaric. Yet peasants, the poor people who lived and farmed in the countryside and made up the vast majority of the population, were routinely executed in the street and their bodies left to rot because they had been accused of not being polite enough to their superiors. The Japanese people lived in much the same way as Europeans had in the time of knights, quests, and sword fights.

## Earliest Western Contact

In 1543, Portuguese merchants "discovered" the Japanese islands while on trading voyages to China. Arriving during the middle of a series of terrible civil wars, the Portuguese brought with them several things that would forever change Japan: Chinese silks, guns, and Christianity.

Oda Nobunaga, known as the Destroyer, was a cruel, brilliant, and crafty leader on one side of the civil war. He used the new guns brought by the Portuguese to help his small army defeat several armies ten times larger. Nobunaga used thousands of guns to terrify his enemy and to pierce their flimsy armor from long distances before attacking in hand-to-hand combat. He never converted to Christianity, but he used it as a tool to fight the power of the Buddhist priests who opposed him. He killed those who would not join him. Entire countrysides were burned, and everyone in them killed simply because the lord of the region had been too slow to obey one of Nobunaga's orders. When Nobunaga died in 1582, he controlled two thirds of Japan.[1]

Toyotomi Hideyoshi, who began his military career as one of Oda Nobunaga's minor officials, rose through the ranks to become his greatest general. He became Nobunaga's successor. Within two years, Hideyoshi killed or made allies of the lords who had opposed Nobunaga. Hideyoshi was known as the Conciliator. He held his alliances together through compromise rather than fear.

With all national power in his hands, Hideyoshi began to change the nation to his liking. He built new roads and bridges. He started a profitable silk trade with China. He made new laws that divided Japanese society into four classes. Warriors called *samurai* were the administrators and military. They were at the top of the hierarchy. Below them were the farmers, the backbone of the country, who fed everyone else. After the farmers were craftsmen. At the bottom were merchants. People remained in the class into which they had been born their whole lives. They were forced to

## Source Document

The Way of the Samurai is found in death. When it comes to either/or, there is only the quick choice of death. When pressed with the choice of life or death, it is not necessary to gain one's aim. We all want to live. And in large part we make our logic according to what we like. But not having attained our aim and continuing to live is cowardice. This is a dangerous thin line. To die without gaining one's aim is a dog's death and fanaticism. But there is no shame in this. This is the substance of the Way of the Samurai. If by setting one's heart right every morning and evening, one is able to live as though his body were already dead, he gains freedom in the Way. His whole life will be without blame, and he will succeed in his calling. . . .[2]

*Before being opened to trade with the West, Japan held many traditions, including a strict division of social classes. This document explains the lifestyle expected of the samurai, or warrior class of Japanese.*

marry within their class. Only the samurai were allowed to have weapons.[3]

In 1600, Tokugawa Ieyasu, an old and crafty ally of both Nobunaga and Hideyoshi, won control of the country at the Battle of Sekigahara. Ieyasu continued to pass laws that kept Japanese society as it was. He began to see the Christians as a threat to his power, because a Christian's first loyalty was to God, not to him. When he commanded a few of his Christian allies to either give up Christianity or leave the country, they chose to leave Japan. In 1614, Ieyasu ordered all foreign priests to leave Japan within a month. All Japanese Christians were ordered to become Buddhists, but not all obeyed. In 1637, a Christian revolt broke out near Nagasaki. After several months, Ieyasu's armies entered the city and killed forty thousand of those who had managed to remain.

For the next two hundred years, everyone in Japan was forced to prove that they were not Christians by registering in a local Buddhist temple. Every man, woman, and child had to walk on pictures of Christ or the Virgin Mary to prove their hatred of Christian values. From that time, a new law proclaimed, "So long as the sun warms the earth, any Christian bold enough to come to Japan . . . even if he be the god of the Christians, shall pay for it with his head."[4]

The family of Tokugawa Ieyasu continued to rule Japan for the next two hundred years. They isolated Japan from foreign influences. Foreign books were forbidden. Japanese citizens were no longer permitted to travel abroad. Laws required Japanese ships to be too small to cross the seas. Unauthorized ships were fired upon when they approached the coast. Shipwrecked foreign sailors were to be killed before they could reach the shore.

The Tokugawa dynasty of rulers was not ignorant of the rest of the world. They were especially impressed with the guns and other modern weapons the industrialized European countries possessed. As a result, the Japanese rulers decided to allow very limited trade with one Western nation. Once a year, the Dutch were allowed to send one ship to trade with the Japanese. The ship could call at only one port, Nagasaki. No foreigners were allowed to visit the city. The Dutch were chosen because, although they were Christians, they were Protestants, not Catholics. They did not try to spread their religion to the Japanese. For the next few hundred years, Japan remained almost completely isolated under the rule of the descendants of Tokugawa Ieyasu.[5]

## The United States Contacts Japan

The first contact between Japan and the United States came soon after American independence from Great Britain. In 1791, during a storm off the coast of Japan, the U.S.S. *Lady Washington*, a merchant ship under the command of Captain John Kendrick, sought shelter in the protected harbors at the eastern end of Japan's Inland Sea. The *Lady Washington* was returning from a trading mission to China. It was carrying

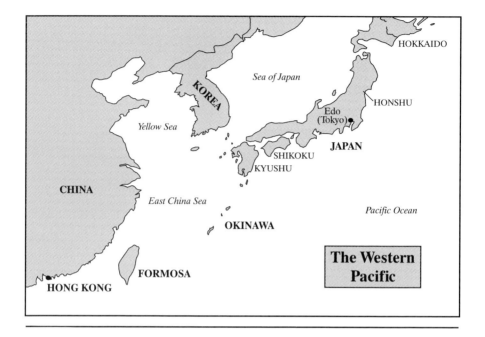

*The western Pacific, including Hong Kong, Formosa, Okinawa, and Japan, was of great strategic importance to the expanding United States.*

furs obtained on the Pacific coast of present-day Oregon. Captain Kendrick knew Japan's policy toward foreigners and he took great care not to arouse Japanese officials. He left a note written in Chinese explaining that he would leave as soon as the storm ended. He did.

During the War of 1812, Captain David Porter of the United States Navy captured twelve British whalers that were cruising in the seas around Japan. In a letter to President James Madison, he recommended that the United States send an expedition to Japan to open that nation to trade. He wrote, "The time may be favorable, and it would be a glory beyond that acquired by any other nation for us, a nation of only forty years standing, to beat down their rooted prejudices, secure to ourselves a valuable trade, and make that people known to the world."[6]

Nothing came of Captain Porter's request at the time. The United States government had no desire to use its few ships and resources for an expedition to a faraway country. Many in the United States at the time wanted to abolish the navy entirely. They considered a navy useless to a small country of farmers and small manufacturers.

During the first years of the nineteenth century, when the nations of Europe were fighting each other, the Dutch were unable to send their ships on trading missions to Japan each year. The Dutch ships feared British warships in the Pacific, and preferred not to fight them. Instead, the Dutch hired merchant ships from the United States to go to Japan for them. Flying the Dutch flag, at least eight American merchant ships visited and traded with Japan between 1797 and 1809.[7]

In 1837, an American businessman in Canton, China, named Charles W. King, wished to open trade with Japan and convert some of the Japanese to Christianity. A few years before, three Japanese sailors had washed up on the coast of Oregon, only to be enslaved by the local American Indians. American merchants bought their freedom, however, and returned them to Canton. The three Japanese sailors waiting in the Chinese port presented King with an opportunity to gain official Japanese acceptance. He evidently forgot that returning the sailors was condemning them to death. Japanese laws against foreigners were so strict that even Japanese citizens who visited other nations were not allowed to return to Japan under penalty of death. King did not believe that the Japanese were at all serious about their laws. He felt that he could violate Japanese laws, since his desire was to bring both more trade and more Christianity to Japan.

King went so far as to remove all the guns from his ship, the U.S.S. *Morrison*, so that Japan would recognize his peaceful intentions. The *Morrison* pulled into Japanese waters near Uraga at the mouth of Tokyo Bay. As soon as the ship anchored, the Japanese began firing cannons from the distant hilltops. The guns were out of range and the shots fell harmlessly into the water. Still, it was not the reception King had hoped for.

No Japanese officials approached the ship, but many small boats soon surrounded the *Morrison*. More than a hundred Japanese fishermen climbed aboard for a look at the strange ship and its foreign crew. To their delight, King gave them small presents and cups of *sake* (rice wine) and cookies. Many stayed until the early hours of the morning. Overnight, however, the Japanese moved their cannons much closer to shore. At daybreak, they began to fire at the ship. Hundreds of small Japanese boats, each carrying a small cannon, attacked the American ship. The

*Morrison* quickly raised its sails and went back out to sea. It had suffered no serious damage. But King had made no contact with Japanese officials, either.

Not content to have escaped unharmed, King and the *Morrison* tried once again. They anchored this time at Kagoshima, a port at the southern tip of Japan. Here, some Japanese officials came aboard and welcomed the foreigners. Two of the returned Japanese sailors went ashore and were taken into custody by officials there. The Japanese told King that, in a couple of days, other, more important, ambassadors would arrive to welcome the Americans. The next day, a fisherman came alongside the ship and warned its crew to leave. King prudently ordered the *Morrison* to withdraw out of the range of any cannons that might be ashore. As the *Morrison* began raising its sails to move, the Japanese on shore saw that the Americans were about to escape the trap they had set. They began firing the many cannons they had hidden near the beach. With the rest of the castaway Japanese sailors still aboard, King returned to Canton. He was outraged at the Japanese deception and his complete failure to open trade relations.

King returned to the United States. In 1839, he wrote a book about his experiences. In it, he noted that the American flag had been fired upon by a foreign government. He concluded that the next move "had better be left to the stronger and wiser action of the American government."[8]

In 1845, a resolution was introduced into the United States Congress. It called for immediate measures to open Japan to trade. Although Congress never approved the measure, the government decided to act anyway. The next year, the government sent two navy ships, one of them carrying seventy-four smooth bore cannons, under the command of Commodore James Biddle, to negotiate with the Japanese.

Biddle anchored his ships in Tokyo Bay in July, the same place that the *Morrison* had first anchored in its unsuccessful attempt at diplomacy. Again, many small rowboats quickly surrounded the American ships. Because he wanted to appear friendly, Biddle did not have them pushed away. In fact, he allowed hundreds of Japanese sightseers to climb aboard his ships to look around. For a week, nothing happened. No official appeared, and every day, more Japanese scrambled aboard for a tour.

Frustrated, Captain Biddle left his ship. He went to a nearby Japanese boat to get some answer to his repeated requests for official recognition. When he tried to board the Japanese boat, he was pushed back into his own boat by one of the Japanese sailors. Biddle was outraged. He immediately demanded that the sailor be arrested. The Japanese laughed at him. He was told that the Japanese only traded with the Dutch. His ship was not welcome in Japanese waters, and perhaps, it would be best for his health if he departed as quickly as possible and did not return. Biddle's pride suffered a final insult when the winds died down and his ships had to be towed out to sea by Japanese rowboats.[9]

## Whalers

Trading with China was one of the reasons that American ships sailed into the western Pacific near Japan. Another reason was whaling. Thousands of whales lived in the waters around Japan. American whalers began hunting there as early as 1788. Whaling quickly became a multimillion-dollar American industry. At the time, whale oil was used to lubricate machinery and burned to provide most American homes with light. More than eighteen thousand men were employed on more than seven hundred ships that searched for whales in the 1830s and 1840s off the coast of Japan.

In June 1848, fifteen sailors from the whaler U.S.S. *Lagoda* deserted their ship, stole several rowboats, and went ashore to Japan. They were quickly surrounded by hundreds of warriors threatening them with long swords, telling them to get back in their boats and leave. When they refused, they were all confined in a large house, which became their prison. After more than a month, several of the men cut a hole in the roof of the house and escaped. There was nowhere for them to run or hide, however, and they were quickly captured again.

After some other prisoners also tried to escape, they were all taken to a Japanese ship and confined in cages below deck. They were taken to Nagasaki and again imprisoned in a large house. Once more, some of them tried to escape. When they were captured, all the prisoners were put in outdoor cages, stripped of their clothing, and given nothing but a mat on which to sleep. During the second night in these cages, one of the men hanged himself. The Japanese left the body swinging in the cage for two days. Another man died frothing at the mouth, delirious from exposure to the rain and snow.

After a time, the Japanese told the prisoners that they were going to cut off their heads. The prisoners told their guards that their country, the United States, would come and free them. This made the guards laugh. The guards told them that common Japanese sailors pushed American commanders around and humiliated them, referring to Commander Biddle. They doubted if any American had the power to tell the Japanese what to do.[10]

## Rescue

Word of the prisoners finally reached an American diplomat in China. He got the news from Dutch traders on their return from their annual trading voyage to Nagasaki. Commander James Glynn sailed his ship, the U.S.S. *Preble*, to Nagasaki to demand the release of the prisoners. Once again, the Japanese refused to cooperate. When the *Preble* anchored, a Japanese boat came alongside with a message. The message told Glynn that everyone should remain aboard the vessel and that no guns should be fired. Glynn threw the message overboard.

Next, an official approached the ship and told Glynn that he would have to anchor outside the harbor. Again, the American ship was surrounded by small Japanese guard boats. Glynn paid no attention. He sailed right through them and anchored in the middle of Nagasaki harbor.

Glynn explained that, if the American prisoners were released to him, he would leave immediately. The Japanese said that any decision had to come from Tokyo. They added that it would take a month or more to get the response, and that foreign sailors were generally released to the Dutch or the Chinese. Glynn accepted no excuses. He kept threatening the Japanese with vague references to what the United States would do if his demands were not met.

The Dutch helped the Americans deal with the Japanese, and after another week, the Japanese delivered the prisoners to the *Preble*. Then the Japanese immediately left before the prisoners could tell the Americans of the horrible treatment they had received. The *Preble* returned to Hong Kong. The prisoners were eventually returned to the United States in 1849. There, their inhumane treatment caused a sensation.[11]

Glynn was the first American to have any success in dealing with the Japanese. He did it by being aggressive and stubborn. Glynn wrote a report in which he stated that he felt Japan was ready for an American diplomatic mission, but that it should be carried out by a powerful naval fleet.[12]

## California, Gold, and the Pacific

Although the public was outraged by the conduct of the Japanese toward the American whalers, there were several other factors that finally turned the attention of the United States government toward Japan. The Mexican War, between the United States and Mexico, had recently ended with an American victory. It brought enormous new lands, including California, into the Union. In 1848, gold was discovered at Sutter's Mill near San Francisco, causing an immediate flood of new emigrants to California.

In 1850, Millard Fillmore became president of the United States. He appointed Daniel Webster as his secretary of state. Both Fillmore and Webster

believed that the United States was destined to become an important world power. One of the ways to accomplish this was for the government to help American businesses expand beyond the borders of the country. Some

*Millard Fillmore, as president, wanted to expand the power of the United States.*

Americans hoped that the United States would eventually acquire new territory, including Cuba, Nicaragua, Panama, and even Mexico. The United States told France to stay away from the Hawaiian Islands, because they were needed for American coaling stations on the way to Asia. England had recently opened markets in China and the United States wanted to have a share in them, too.

At this time, the United States was driven by the concept of Manifest Destiny. Many Americans believed that the United States should expand to include territory from the Atlantic to Pacific coasts of North America, as well as other places around the globe. The Industrial Revolution, which was helping the United States become a nation of factories and manufacturers, in addition to traditional farmers, sparked a need for new markets for American products. Asia seemed a perfect place for such an expansion of trade, especially since many Americans at the time held racist attitudes that considered Asians inferior to whites of European background. Americans believed they werc divinely supported in their attempts to expand across the continent and in the world of trade.

American businessmen who established steamship lines in the Pacific received $200,000 a year from the United States government.[13] In 1851, Congress voted another $874,000 to put more American steamships in the Pacific. The House of Representatives committee on naval affairs sponsored a measure to loan a Philadelphia businessman $5 million to establish six mail steamships between California and China. That same year, Secretary of the Navy William Graham asked for $8.1 million for the navy. He noted that the United States had established a new presence in the Pacific that required a rear admiral and a fleet that would encourage and protect American business ventures in Asia.[14] These ventures would include a mission to try to begin trade with Japan.

The government considered several high-ranking naval officers to lead the Asian mission. The commander of such an expedition would need courage, independence, self-reliance, diplomatic experience, and patience. It would also not hurt if the new commander were someone who was used to getting his way. Matthew Calbraith Perry was all this and more. He was perfect for the job. In January 1852, Perry was ordered to report to Washington, D.C.

# Chapter 3

# Matthew Perry, the Soul of the United States Navy

The first Perrys to move to America were Edward Perry and his family. The Perrys left England and settled on Cape Cod in the Massachusetts Bay Colony around 1639. Almost all of their neighbors were Puritans who treated the Perrys badly because they were Quakers. Edward Perry soon moved his family to the more isolated and tolerant Rhode Island colony. They settled in a large home, called Wakefield, on the western shore of Narragansett Bay.

## The Perry Family History

Over the next hundred years, the Perrys thrived. They established dairy farms and raised fine horses. Matthew's grandfather, Freeman Perry, was the town doctor of South Kingston, its land surveyor, and chief justice of the county court. When the American

Revolution began, Christopher Perry, Freeman's son, joined the local militia in support of the American patriots.

Christopher served on several ships that raided British merchant ships. The British captured and imprisoned him twice, once in New York and once in Ireland. While he was imprisoned in Ireland, he fell in love with the young daughter of the prison commandant and vowed to marry her. Before he was even able to speak to her, however, he had a chance to escape and took it.

Soon after the American Revolution ended with an American victory, Christopher Perry returned to Dublin aboard a merchant ship. There, standing on the dock, he saw the girl he had seen at the prison several years before, Sarah Wallace Alexander. She was waiting to board a ship bound for Philadelphia. Christopher lost little time in introducing himself. Without much thought, he decided to go with her to Philadelphia. By the time the ship arrived, Christopher had proposed to and been accepted by Sarah Alexander.

The new couple settled in Newport, Rhode Island, and Christopher returned to sea as a merchant captain. Oliver Hazard Perry, their first son, was born in August 1785. Raymond followed in 1789, and Sarah Wallace was born in 1791. Matthew Calbraith Perry, their fourth child, was born in Newport, Rhode Island, on April 10, 1794. He would be called Calbraith by his family and friends.[1] After Matthew, four Perry children followed. Anna Marie was born in 1797, Jane in 1799, James in 1801, and Nathaniel in 1802.

Little is known of Matthew's early life at home. His mother, Sarah, served as both mother and father to the children during Christopher's long absences. The children learned to read and write from their mother, but they spent most of the day playing and doing chores around the house. As soon as they were old enough, the young boys went to sea. The Perrys were a seagoing family.

In 1798, the new United States began an unofficial war with France. Christopher Perry was given command of the U.S.S. *General Greene*, a 124-foot-long frigate carrying thirty-two cannons. Oliver Hazard Perry, Christopher's thirteen-year-old eldest son, signed on as part of the crew. The United States government sent the *General Greene* and the Perrys to the island of Hispaniola in the Caribbean Sea in support of Toussaint L'Ouverture, who was leading a revolt against the French in the colony of Haiti.

*Oliver Hazard Perry, Matthew's older brother, would become a military hero.*

After succeeding in his assignment to Haiti, Christopher Perry retired from the navy. Oliver, however, was sent to the Mediterranean Sea. There, pirates from Tripoli were raiding American ships. The United States government decided to go to war with Tripoli to stop the pirates. It was a successful campaign that made many nations respect the rights of American ships at sea.

Oliver Hazard Perry performed so well in these operations that he was given his first command in 1809 aboard the *Revenge*, a small schooner carrying twelve guns. One of the first acts Oliver performed as the new commander was to enlist his fifteen-year-old brother, Matthew, to serve under his command. Matthew was next transferred to a new forty-four-gun frigate, U.S.S. *President*, to serve under Commodore John Rodgers.

Perry had had no formal education. He was educated in the knowledge of his career by the other officers onboard ship. How good an education each midshipman received depended upon the whim of the commanding officer and the desire of the midshipman to learn. Matthew took great pride in learning. He read extensively and became an amateur scientist.

## The War of 1812

Ever since the French Revolution in 1789, England had been at war with France, and desperately needed men for the infantry regiments that fought battles all over Europe. The English also needed men for the many ships of their mighty navy. The British Navy was the best in the world. It had more than six hundred fighting ships.

The United States Navy consisted of only sixteen ships. The British felt that the tiny new nation of the United States was hardly ready to stand up to the mightiest navy in the world. British ships began to wait off the American coast. They would attack and stop American ships, kidnap most of their English-speaking sailors, and then sail to attack French ships off the coast of Europe.

The United States government decided that it had to fight the British to stop this practice, called impress-ment. Matthew Calbraith Perry first saw action in May 1811 when the *President* attacked and defeated the British sloop H.M.S. *Little Belt* near Chesapeake Bay. The next year, the United States formally declared war against Great Britain, starting the War of 1812.

After the *Little Belt* incident, Commodore Rodgers commanded three other cruisers in the Atlantic, look-ing for British ships. Although Rodgers's ships captured several British merchantmen, they saw no real action. The British soon turned many of their heavier warships to the American front and success-fully blockaded the Atlantic harbors of the Americans by August 1813. Rodgers and Perry spent the rest of the war aboard a ship anchored in New York Harbor.

Matthew Perry used his time in New York to court the daughter of John Slidell, a wealthy merchant, banker, and ship owner. On Christmas Eve, 1814, the

*The U.S.S.* President *was the ship on which Matthew Perry had his first combat experience.*

day the Treaty of Ghent was signed to end the war, twenty-year-old Matthew Perry married seventeen-year-old Jane Slidell.

## Pirates of Algiers

The United States defended its international rights against the might of Great Britain in the War of 1812, but there were still other nations of the world that tried to take advantage of the young nation. The dey of Algiers was one of the most powerful pirate princes on the Barbary Coast (the Mediterranean Sea coast of Africa). He had been capturing American ships and enslaving the sailors. He did not reply to diplomatic protests. So the United States declared war on Algiers shortly after the War of 1812 was over.

The United States sent two squadrons of ships against the African nation. Matthew Perry left Boston Harbor on July 3, 1815, as the second in command of the U.S.S. *Chippewa*. By the time the *Chippewa* reached the Mediterranean Sea, it was no longer needed. Captain Stephen Decatur had arrived with his fleet, promptly captured the flagship of the prince of the Barbary Coast, and forced him to free the enslaved American sailors and sign a peace treaty.

Both Perry's and Decatur's fleets sailed along the Barbary Coast and made threatening approaches to the ships in Tunis and Tripoli harbors, to remind the pirates of American sea power. They left four ships to protect American shipping, then the rest of the ships sailed for home. They arrived in Newport, Rhode Island, on November 15, 1815.

It had been an exciting adventure for Perry. Not only did he fight pirates, but he had taught himself Spanish and translated a Spanish book on the navigation of the Mediterranean. He also learned the value of a strong navy to protect the rights of American citizens in the world of international politics. When Perry returned to the United States, he would use his influence among his extended navy family to get a new assignment.

There were more officers than jobs available on the few American ships still on duty after the War of

1812. Assignments and promotions within the navy were given by the Navy Department's board of commissioners in Washington, D.C. The board at this time was headed by John Rodgers, Perry's commander aboard the U.S.S. *President* and a family friend. Perry's sister, Anna Maria, married George Rodgers, the younger brother of John Rodgers. With his family connections, even when most naval officers were released from duty, Matthew Perry continued to hold important positions.[2]

On August 3, 1819, twenty-five-year-old Matthew Perry received a commission as the first lieutenant aboard the U.S.S. *Cyane*. The *Cyane* was a small light ship with only a few cannons that had been captured from the British in the recent war. It carried a crew of one hundred eighty men. The first lieutenant was the second in command of the ship and a promotion for Perry.[3]

## Freed Slaves on the Coast of Africa

Ever since slavery first began in America, people had argued over whether slavery were right and what should be done with slaves if and when they were freed. Many people wanted to return freed slaves to their homelands in Africa. As early as 1773, there was a plan in Newport, Rhode Island, to send freed slaves back to Africa. The British began to send homeless Africans in England to a colony in Sierra Leone beginning in 1787. Paul Cuffee, a wealthy freed African man in Massachusetts, brought thirty-eight freed slaves to the colony in Sierra Leone in 1815. He died before he could return to the colony with more.

Early in 1817, Henry Clay of Kentucky, John Randolph of Virginia, and other political leaders in the United States founded the American Colonization Society. It was dedicated to sending freed slaves to Africa. Henry Clay used his influence as a senator to have the United States government give $100,000 to the American Colonization Society. The society rented a ship and hired a crew to return freed slaves to Africa in Sierra Leone. The United States government would direct its ship *Cyane* to offer the ship its protection and help in African waters. The *Cyane* was also to patrol the waters off the African coast in search of illegal slave ships.

Great Britain outlawed the importation of slaves into its territory in 1807. The United States did so in 1808. The American law that forbade the importation of slaves also provided that any ships found engaged in the slave trade were to be seized and sold at auction in an American port. Most, but not all, European countries joined England and the United States in a treaty that outlawed the slave trade in 1815. At that time, Spain had not outlawed the trade in slaves and many slave ships flew the Spanish flag so that they would not be taken by American or British ships patrolling African waters.

The *Cyane* met the U.S.S. *Elizabeth*, the ship that actually carried the colonists to Africa, at the colony in Sierra Leone in March 1820. The crew saw the new immigrants get off the ship. It was a terrible scene. Local natives constantly attacked the freed slaves. They regarded them as foreign invaders. The British who governed the Sierra Leone colony also looked at the new American colonists as invaders. The British made them live on swampy nearby Sherbro Island. The rainy season had just started and everything was flooded. Mosquitoes were everywhere. Yellow fever killed more than one third of the new colonists within six months.

After the *Cyane* left the colonists, it continued to sail along the coast, seeking illegal slave ships. On April 10, 1820, it captured a fleet of seven ships. Though they flew the Spanish flag, they were actually ships from New York, Baltimore, and Charleston. These ships were taken by the *Cyane* as prizes of the United States. With one or two of the *Cyane*'s junior officers aboard each ship to direct the crew, they sailed back across the Atlantic Ocean to be sold at auction.

During the same trip to Africa, the *Cyane* also found two ships filled with slaves ready for the passage across the Atlantic. These ships were taken, the crews jailed, and the ships burned. The slaves were freed and sent to the British colony in Sierra Leone.

At the nearby harbor of Cape Mesurado, Perry noted the rich lands, few swamps, and the friendly natives of the area who did not deal in slaves. He requested permission from the local tribes to have the

American colonists now at Sierra Leone move there to settle. The natives agreed.

## Perry's First Command

The *Cyane* reached the United States on Christmas, 1820. Perry returned to New York and his family for a long, happy vacation. On July 21, 1821, Perry was ordered to Washington, D.C. There, he took command of the new armed schooner U.S.S. *Shark*.

Perry loved his first command. Eighty-six-feet long, carrying a crew of seventy and twelve guns, the *Shark* was fast and sat high out of the water. It was a delight to sail.

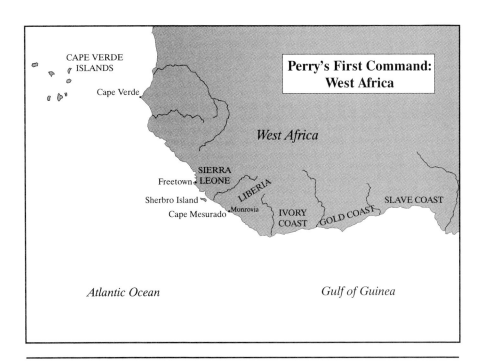

*The west coast of Africa was the scene of Perry's first command.*

Perry's orders directed him to bring Reverend Eli Ayers, the United States commissioner, to the new colony at Cape Mesurado and then continue to search for slave ships. After a quick sail to Africa, Ayers promptly contacted the nearby tribal chiefs and formally bought the site of Monrovia, Liberia, for an assortment of axes, hatchets, cloth, and other trading goods. The first of the Sierra Leone survivors arrived in the new colony on January 7, 1822.

Perry's *Shark* then proceeded to hunt for slave ships. It captured a French slave ship loaded with a thousand gallons of rum, seven thousand pounds of tobacco, and a trunk full of umbrellas its owners had intended to trade for slaves. Perry had to let the ship go, because there were no slaves aboard. Later, he overtook another French slave ship with more than one hundred thirty slaves aboard. Because France had not signed the international agreement to suppress the slave trade, Perry was forced to let the ship go, as well.

In November 1821, the *Shark* crossed the Atlantic without meeting any suspicious ships and reached the tropical waters off the coast of Cuba, which was then a colony of Spain. Perry sent several small boats with crews up the rivers, looking for pirates who preyed on merchant ships in the area. Perry caught a small boatload of pirates and sent them to the Spanish governor general of Cuba for trial and a swift hanging.

In Kingston, Jamaica, Perry received orders to return to New York immediately. Fighting a winter storm most of the way, the *Shark* arrived in New York

Harbor in December 1821, totally coated with ice. Perry and his men arrived just in time for a well-deserved Christmas vacation.[4]

## Family Life

For the next ten years, Matthew Perry spent most of his time away from his home, mainly in the Mediterranean Sea. The long separations led to many joyful reunions with his wife, Jane. Together, they had ten children. Nearly every time Matthew Perry returned from one of his assignments at sea, Jane Perry became pregnant. Their first son, John, was born in 1816. Sarah was born in 1818, followed by Jane in 1819. Matthew Calbraith, Jr., was born in 1821, and daughter Susan in 1824. Oliver Hazard Perry II was born in 1825, William Frederick in 1828, Caroline in 1829, Isabella in 1834, and Anna, the last of the Perry children, was born in 1838.

Three of the Perry children died in infancy: John when he was twelve months old, Susan at fifteen months, and the youngest, Anna, died before she was a year old. Matthew Perry was devoted to his children and asked to be buried next to his infant Anna upon his death.

## A Turkish Pasha

On July 26, 1824, Perry was made second in command of the battleship U.S.S. *North Carolina*. Its mission was to guard American shipping in the Aegean Sea during the war that was going on between Greece and Turkey.

Perry and the Americans quickly negotiated with the Greeks, who agreed to leave American ships alone, but they were unable to reach the Turkish admiral. By chance the next summer, while on an assignment to aid a beached Turkish ship, Perry met the Lord High Admiral Capudan Pasha. The Pasha, third in rank of the entire Ottoman Empire (as the area controlled by Turkey was then called), and Perry became friends. The Pasha said he would be delighted to meet with the Americans for a conference.

When the meeting took place on July 14, 1825, the *North Carolina* gave the Pasha a twenty-one-gun salute. All the American sailors, dressed in their best white uniforms, gave the Pasha three cheers. The Turks and the Americans quickly came to an agreement. After his success in negotiating with the Pasha, Perry was often called to act as a diplomat, meeting with foreign leaders.

## Dealing With a Pompous Fool

On April 22, 1830, Matthew Perry was ordered to take command of the U.S.S. *Concord*, a brand new sloop-of-war. His first mission was to bring John Randolph, a new ambassador from the United States, to Russia. Randolph was from an old, aristocratic Virginia family. He was used to having everyone around him obey his slightest whim. Perry's orders were to do whatever Randolph wanted. Randolph knew this, and for several months, he used the *Concord* as his personal ship and Perry as his chauffeur. As captain of a sailing ship,

Perry was not used to having anyone tell him what to do. This mission sorely tested Perry's patience. Nevertheless, Perry was always polite and tolerated Randolph's insults and demands.

Randolph finally left the ship on August 11, 1830, at Kronstadt, Russia. However, he instructed Perry to wait for some letters he wanted to have delivered as soon as possible. Perry waited and waited. Finally, on August 22, Randolph and all his baggage returned. St. Petersburg was too hot, too dusty, and had too many insects for him. He directed Perry to return him to England, where he would spend the winter. "Ambassador" Randolph never returned to Russia. His trip had cost the government $16,000, almost fifteen years' salary for Perry.[5]

## Bay of Naples, 1832

The Kingdom of the Two Sicilies, a group of small states in southern Italy and Sicily, owed the United States a debt because it had interfered with American shipping during the wars of the early nineteenth century. By July 1832, John Nelson, the American ambassador at Naples, the capital of the kingdom, determined that the only way the debt would be paid was through the use of force. He suggested that perhaps the American government should accept a number of valuable artworks as payment for the debt. The government refused. It wanted cash.

The government placed the United States Navy in charge of collecting the debt. Perry was promoted to

*Matthew Perry, as he looked as a young naval officer.*

the rank of acting commodore. He was given orders to lead the Mediterranean squadron into the Bay of Naples and demand the money.[6] This type of mission was quickly becoming second nature to Perry. He chose the newest, best frigate in the navy, the U.S.S. *Brandywine*, for his flagship. He silently sailed to the Bay of Naples, along with the frigate *Constellation* and the sloops *John Adams* and *Boston*. The people of Naples quickly began to fortify the town and tried to negotiate with the American ambassador.

Perry entertained army officials and the royalty of the kingdom aboard his flagship. He held formal dinners, dances, and many champagne toasts. Visitors were allowed to inspect the cannons and well-disciplined gun crews as the ship's band played the latest dances under the stars. On October 14, 1832, the mission paid off. The king agreed to pay the United States 2 million ducats (currency) within nine years. Perry sailed for home.

For twenty straight days, Perry's ship battled fierce Atlantic winter storms as it hurried to deliver the news of the American success to President Andrew Jackson. The ship pulled into Portsmouth, New Hampshire, on December 4. It took a couple of weeks for the crew to be dismissed and the ship's equipment and rigging stored. Matthew Perry then left the ship and returned to his family in New York City. He had been absent for two years.

## Years Ashore

Perry spent most of the next ten years on land. He was appointed commander of the navy recruiting station in New York in January 1833. Perry was happy ashore. It gave him a chance to catch up with his growing family.

In 1837, Perry supervised the construction of the navy's first steamship, the U.S.S. *Fulton*, named after the man who put the first commercial steamboat into operation. The *Fulton* was one hundred eighty feet long with two engines that operated paddlewheels on the sides of the ship.

It was a strange sight to old-fashioned sailors, but it was the image of the future. Perry immediately saw the potential of a ship that was not dependent upon the winds and tides to go where it wanted. In May 1838, he sailed the *Fulton* to Washington, D.C. There, it was inspected and approved by President Martin Van Buren.

An entirely new kind of sailor was needed to work with the new steamship, a knowledgeable engineer. Perry not only created the standards and pay scale for these new navy engineers, but he also worked to encourage the navy to start training its own engineers. Partly through Perry's efforts, the United States Navy set up the Naval Academy at Annapolis, Maryland, on October 10, 1845.[7]

## War With Mexico

The United States made Texas, a former Mexican territory, part of the Union in 1845. For years, there were

*The Naval Academy at Annapolis, which Matthew Perry helped establish, is seen here as it looked in 1853.*

many disputes between the United States and Mexico about the southern boundary of Texas. General Zachary Taylor was sent to the area along the Rio Grande to protect American interests there. In May 1846, Mexican soldiers unsuccessfully attacked General Taylor. The United States then declared war on Mexico.

The United States Navy in the Caribbean Sea, a substantial force that included the steamships *Mississippi* and *Princeton*, under the command of Commodore David Connor, soon began a blockade of Mexican ports. There was no Mexican Navy, so there was no one to oppose the American blockade.

*General Zachary Taylor led American troops during the Mexican War.*

In August 1846, Perry was ordered to deliver two small steamships to the blockading fleet and then take command of the U.S.S. *Mississippi.* He arrived in September.

In mid-November, American naval forces attacked Tampico, Mexico. When the armed sailors appeared, the town surrendered.

Perry and the *Mississippi* steamed to Brownsville, Texas, to pick up army personnel, then to New Orleans, Louisiana, where Perry picked up guns and tools. Perry returned the men and supplies to Tampico in only a week. This amazed the navy chiefs. They now saw the advantages of the fast steamships in war. Perry was promoted to commodore. He relieved Commodore Connor of the command of the entire American fleet on March 21, 1847.

The Mexican government, although severely out-gunned, refused to surrender. The United States government decided that the only way to win the war was to send another army to attack Mexico City. The United States decided to support General Zachary Taylor's invasion from the north with another invasion

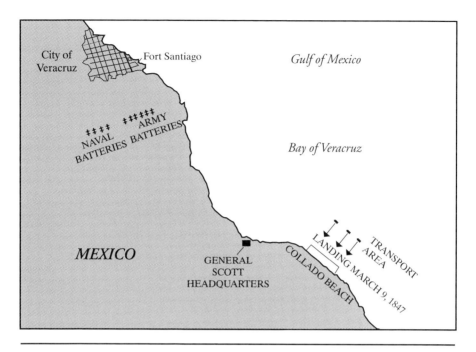

City of Veracruz

Fort Santiago

*Gulf of Mexico*

NAVAL BATTERIES

ARMY BATTERIES

*Bay of Veracruz*

*MEXICO*

GENERAL SCOTT HEADQUARTERS

COLLADO BEACH

LANDING AREA

TRANSPORT

MARCH 9, 1847

*Perry played a role in the siege of Veracruz during the Mexican War.*

from the east. The navy was directed to help General Winfield Scott's army land near Veracruz.

Once Scott's forces had successfully landed, they marched to the port city and ordered its surrender. Stationed behind the thick walls that surrounded the town, the Mexicans refused. Scott's artillery was not powerful enough to blow holes in the thick walls.

Scott asked Perry to lend him the navy's more powerful Paixhan guns to break through the walls. Perry insisted that his own men would go with the guns and operate them after the army engineers had prepared suitable foundations for the heavy weapons. Scott agreed. He saw that he would be unable to defeat the town without the navy's help.

Perry took six eight-inch guns and their mounts from aboard ship and had them brought to the beach at night. There, they were dragged three miles to foundations prepared by Captain Robert E. Lee. After four days of bombardment, large holes were blown in the walls. The Mexican general of the town surrendered. The road to Mexico City, the capital, was open. Perry organized the marines of his troops into a regiment and sent them with General Scott's army to take the Mexican capital.

In June 1847, Perry sailed up the Coatzacoalcos River to the town of Tabasco. With small steamships, he captured the town in fierce hand-to-hand fighting. He wanted to hold Tabasco until peace talks could take place. The negotiations would involve the issue of building a canal between the Atlantic and Pacific oceans across the Isthmus of Tehuantepec. General Scott entered Mexico

*Robert E. Lee, who later became a Confederate general during the American Civil War, was a hero of the Mexican War.*

# Source Document

## Article V

The Boundary line between the two Republics shall commence in the Gulf of Mexico, three leagues from land, opposite the mouth of the Rio Grande, otherwise called Rio Bravo del Norte, or opposite the mouth of it's deepest branch, if it should have more than one branch emptying directly into the sea; from thence, up the middle of that river, following the deepest channel, where it has more than one to the point where it strikes the Southern boundary of New Mexico; thence, westwardly along the whole Southern Boundary of New Mexico (which runs north of the town called Paso) to it's western termination; thence, northward, along the western line of New Mexico, until it intersects the first branch of the river Gila; (or if it should not intersect any branch of that river, then, to the point on the said line nearest to such branch, and thence in a direct line to the same;) thence down the middle of the said branch and of the said river, until it empties into the Rio Colorado; thence, across the Rio Colorado, following the division line between Upper and Lower California, to the Pacific Ocean.[8]

*The Mexican War, which ended with the signing of the Treaty of Guadalupe-Hidalgo, gave the United States a great deal of new territory in the West, and settled the boundaries between Mexico and the United States.*

City on September 17, 1847. The city's surrender ended the war.[9]

Matthew Perry returned to New York in July 1848 a hero. He was now the most famous man in the United States Navy. His fame would help lead to new missions, including his historic trip to Japan.

# Chapter 4

# Perry's First Visit to the Empire of Japan

Matthew Perry's Black Fleet arrived in Japan in July 1853. When it appeared that the American ships had no intention of following the Japanese order to leave, Kayama and Nakajima, two harbor policemen, tied their boats together and talked over the situation.

It soon became apparent that at least one man on both the American and Japanese sides could speak and understand Dutch. Nakajima had brought an interpreter in his boat. Speaking Dutch, the interpreter asked the Americans who they were, how powerful their guns were, and whether they knew that they were violating the laws of Japan by being there. The Americans ignored the questions. They stated that they were following the laws of the United States.

*A Japanese artist drew this portrait of Commodore Matthew Perry.*

# Confrontation

The Americans demanded to be allowed to present a letter from the United States president to a high Japanese official. In response, Nakajima said he was the vice governor of Uraga, and asked to speak to an American officer of similar rank. When Perry was told of Nakajima's request to come aboard, he agreed. However, he told his officers that he wanted them to make the Japanese wait for a while first.

Nakajima came aboard the *Susquehanna* with his interpreter. At his waist, he carried two swords. Over his black shirt and pants, he wore a black cloak embroidered in golden thread with the emblem of the Tokugawa coat of arms—three hollyhock leaves pointing inward from a circular border. Nakajima was an impressive figure.

He was presented to Lieutenant John Contee. The two men talked for a time. Nakajima insisted that the harbor at Nagasaki, Japan, was the only place foreign ships were allowed. All letters must be exchanged there. Contee replied that Commodore Perry expected to be received where he had anchored—here, in Tokyo Bay. Contee then informed Nakajima that, although the Americans had come in peace, they would not allow the many small Japanese guard boats to remain so close to the ship. The Americans were prepared to drive the boats away by force, if necessary.

Nakajima rose immediately. He went to the guardrail of the *Susquehanna*'s main deck, and in a loud voice, ordered all the Japanese boats to depart. They did.

When Nakajima returned, Contee told him that the Americans were prepared to deliver the president's letter themselves to the emperor in Tokyo if no suitable government official were prepared to receive Commodore Perry. Nakajima must have been disturbed by the idea of United States military men marching through the streets of Tokyo to the palace of the shogun. When Contee asked him whether he would like to be responsible for such a disgrace, Nakajima said no. He told the American that a more powerful official would arrive from Tokyo the next day. Before he left, Nakajima carefully inspected the ship's huge Paixhan gun that was aimed at the town of Uraga less than a mile away. Commodore Perry wrote in his journal with some satisfaction, "The first important point is gained."[1]

## Panic in the Streets

The first official reports written by Nakajima and Kayama about the Americans reached Tokyo by an express boat after dark. The Bakufu, or government bureaucracy, took immediate precautions. It declared a national state of emergency and moved the army to protect the palace of the shogun.

Rumors of the American ships quickly spread from town to town. Soon, the news had been heard throughout Tokyo. Families hid their valuables and food. Many started to leave the city, carrying all they could on their backs. People flocked to the shrines to pray. Temple bells rang out all over the town.

The outlying army units were given orders to march to the coast, ready to repel the foreign invaders. They marched in formation accompanied by flags, silk banners, and huge drums that were mounted on wheels and sounded out the beat for the marching soldiers. The army completely blocked the roads. People fleeing from coastal fishing villages found it hard to move. It was a scene of mass confusion.[2]

## Surveying the Harbor

Aboard the American ships, the sailors spent the night in quiet readiness. The ships' boilers were kept fully stoked. The men remained at their stations, ready to repel boarders or fire the cannons if needed. Nothing happened. The night passed in peace.

Early the next morning, even before the fog had completely lifted, the Americans lowered a number of small boats into the water. Their crews began to survey the harbor. The United States had no accurate maps of these coastal waters. The Japanese kept even the names of the local fishing villages secret from the Americans. If there were going to be trouble, Commodore Perry needed to know where the enemy guns were located and where he could sail his ships without getting stuck on the bottom. His ordering the survey was an outrageous act. It could best be compared with the idea of a visitor to one's home sticking his or her nose into all the cabinets and drawers. But there was little the outgunned Japanese could do.

There were two governors of the district of Uraga. When one of them, Toda Izu, saw what the Americans were doing in the harbor, he sent Kayama and two interpreters to the *Susquehanna*. Kayama's cloak was made of silk and embroidered with a peacock in gold and silver thread.

Kayama introduced himself to the Americans as one of the governors of Uraga. It was a lie that exaggerated his importance. Kayama asked the Americans the same questions Nakajima had asked the night before. He was given the same reply: Commodore Perry wanted to deliver a letter to the emperor.

Kayama then asked what the American small boats were doing in the harbor. He was told that they were surveying. That was illegal under Japanese law, Kayama replied. Lieutenant Contee told him that American law required its navy to survey unknown harbors. Kayama let the matter drop for the moment.

Kayama then informed the Americans that he was going to leave. He would return in four days with further orders from Tokyo. The Americans protested. Four days was too long. Tokyo was only a few hours away. Commodore Perry expected an official answer within three days—by July 12, 1853. There would be no further communication until that official reply.[3]

Perry was encouraged by the first reports of the sailors who had conducted the survey of the harbor early that morning. They had found that Japanese

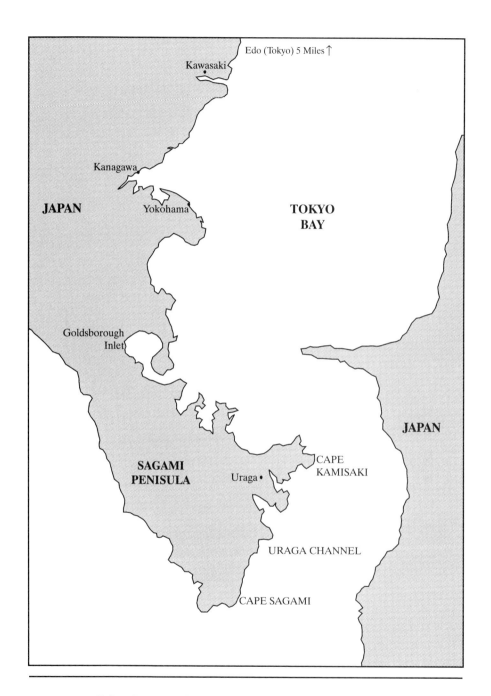

*Tokyo Bay was the scene of Perry's two visits to Japan.*

defenses were poor. The crews could count only fourteen guns, none of them large enough to threaten an American ship. They had also found that the coastal fortifications south of Uraga were fake and that there was a channel deep enough for the American ships to move around. Their good position meant they could afford to be stubborn with the Japanese. That night, Perry noted in his journal that carrying out the survey was "a second and most important point gained."[4]

Kayama left the *Susquehanna* and reported back to Toda Izu, the governor who had sent him to the ship. By 2:00 P.M., Kayama was headed for the capital, where he would discuss his impressions of the intruders with Ido Iwami, the highest governor of Uraga District and Toda Izu's boss. Ido Iwami was a prince, a member of an old warrior family that had voluntarily joined the Tokugawa family to rule the country centuries before. He was an important official.

The Bakufu met the next morning. Ido Iwami gave everyone the news—there was a well-armed American fleet anchored within twenty-eight miles of Tokyo, threatening to send troops to deliver a letter to the emperor. The Bakufu could not decide what to do. The law said that the foreigners must be attacked and driven away. Some Japanese officials wanted to do that. Most, however, thought it would be suicide.

Finally, the Japanese took no action. They simply continued the debate, knowing they had several more days to decide what to do. In the meantime, they gave control of the situation to Toda Izu back in Uraga.

By 3:00 P.M. on Sunday, July 10, Kayama was headed back to Uraga. He had with him orders for Toda Izu to deal with the Americans. His instructions said to make every effort to make them leave peacefully and take the American president's letter to Nagasaki instead of trying to force the Japanese to receive it in Tokyo Bay.[5]

## Another Confrontation

Early Monday morning, July 11, the American survey boats were back in the water. The crews continued to explore the Japanese waters, this time farther inland toward Tokyo. Perry sent the *Mississippi* along to protect the survey boats. The *Mississippi*, with its cannons loaded and ready, followed slowly behind.

Later in the morning, the survey boats rounded a point of land called Kannonsaki that separated the outer from the inner harbors. When Toda Izu saw that the *Mississippi* was slowly steaming toward Tokyo, he immediately sent Nakajima to try and stop the American boats. He also ordered Kayama to go to the *Susquehanna* to find out what was happening.

After he asked a casual question about the *Mississippi* and the survey boats, the Americans told Kayama that, if Perry did not receive a satisfactory response about his demands, the Americans would have to return the next spring with a larger fleet. Just in case this happened, the Americans said, the survey boats were searching for a suitable anchorage closer to Tokyo.

In the harbor, the survey boats passed out of the sight of both the *Mississippi* and the *Susquehanna*. As they continued their work near the shore, they were approached by a number of Japanese guard boats. The Japanese sailors motioned for the survey boats to return to their mother ship. The survey boats were equipped with brass cannons loaded with grapeshot. They simply ignored the Japanese and pressed on with their work. The Japanese boats appeared to be unarmed.

Finally, the American boats were confronted by a line of forty or so guard boats that stopped them from going any farther. The American sailors were ordered to fix their bayonets to their muskets and wait. Their boats nose to nose, the two sides sat unmoving and silent. Then, one of the survey boats rowed back around Kannonsaki point to call the *Mississippi* back. Soon, the big ship came slowly up behind the survey boats, passed lines to them, and slowly towed them back. It had been a dangerous confrontation. Neither side had really wanted any violence. Commodore Perry had only wanted to scare the Japanese a little more.[6]

## Success

Perry had succeeded in scaring the Japanese when he moved the *Mississippi*. Reports that an American warship had passed Kannonsaki only added to the general confusion and feeling of helplessness among the Japanese. In Tokyo, army units were lined up all along

## Source Document

The Commodore had previously to the arrival of the governor, written the following letter to the Emperor:—

To his Imperial Majesty the Emperor of Japan.

The Commander-in-chief of the United States naval forces in these seas, being invested with full powers to negotiate treaties, is desirous of conferring with one of the highest officers of the Empire of Japan, in view of making arrangements for the presentation of the original of his letter of credence, as also the original of a letter with which he is charged, addressed to his Imperial Majesty by the President of the United States.

It is hope that an early day will be appointed for the proposed interview.[7]

*In the official report of the expedition, Perry later explained how he initially tried to begin negotiations with the Japanese.*

the waterfront. The Bakufu ordered that the city's temple bells be rung when the Americans landed. When this order became known, it only confirmed everyone's fears that the Americans would soon arrive. Rice and other foods quickly became unavailable. All the secondhand swords and guns in the capital were sold.

The head of the Bakufu, Abe Masahiro, finally had to tell the sick and dying shogun, Ieyoshi Tokugawa, about the potential American invasion. Masahiro knew that the Japanese officials had to accept the American letter. Even so, it was not until after midnight on July 12 that he arranged for the Bakufu to agree formally to accept President Millard Fillmore's letter.

The Bakufu ordered Ido Iwami and Toda Izu to accept the letter in a way that would preserve Japan's honor. They were also to try to avoid problems in the future. They drafted a letter to Perry. It introduced Prince Ido Iwami and Toda Izu as the high public officials who would receive the Americans' letter.[8]

At 9:30 A.M. on July 12, Kayama returned to the *Susquehanna* with word of the Bakufu's decision. The letter would soon be accepted. The Bakufu said it would be accepted near Uraga. However, the Japanese wanted the Americans to receive their response at Nagasaki, not where they now were. The Chinese or the Dutch would deliver the response, rather than the Japanese.

From his stateroom below decks, Matthew Perry replied to Kayama in writing. He said he had no intention of going to Nagasaki to wait for the reply. Nor would he accept a reply through Chinese or Dutch representatives. Furthermore, Perry would not hold himself accountable for the consequences if the Japanese continued to insult the president of the United States.

The junior American officers and Kayama spent several hours that day and most of the next day deciding exactly how the exchange of the letter would occur. They planned for the letter to be handed over early on the morning of July 14 on the shores of a nearby bay named Kurihama, which lay in view of the ships south of Uraga. It was a natural setting with a beautiful beach. The spot was satisfactory to both the Japanese Army and the American gunners aboard the ships.

Perry was to bring exactly two hundred fifty men with him. The Japanese officials who were to receive the letter were named. The man who was actually to receive the letter in his hands, Toda Izu, was not allowed to enter into any form of discussion with the Americans. He would remain silent during the exchange.[9]

## Preparing for the Meeting

All night long, sounds of activity filled the air. From the decks of the American ships, carpenters could be heard until the early hours of the morning, hammering and sawing on the beach at Kurihama. Below decks on the American ships, there was fevered activity. The men who had been chosen to go ashore with Commodore Perry by a lottery that last evening were polishing their shoes and swords. Each sailor, dressed in blue trousers and a white cotton shirt, was given a musket and twenty rounds of ball cartridges. They were to look good, but they were also to be prepared in case trouble arose. The officers dressed in their fanciest uniforms and carried polished swords and Colt revolvers.

Before dawn, the American steamships fired up their boilers and began to move. Slowly, the big black ships moved to where their guns covered the Kurihama beach and anchored. Small boats were lowered from the decks. Some would carry Commodore Perry and the two hundred fifty men of his escort ashore. Others were armed with small cannons. They would be held in reserve in case of trouble.

As the mist of the morning disappeared, the Americans could see what seemed to be a magical transformation. All along the beach, a canvas screen in sections eight- to ten-feet high had been raised. It made the entire beach look like a stage. In front of the screens were four to five thousand Japanese Army soldiers clustered around their military banners and flags. They were dressed in armor and carried spears, swords, and ancient matchlock rifles.

Behind them stood mounted cavalry units, their officers dressed in gaily embroidered silk gowns. At one end of the beach were three large canvas tents.

They looked like a scene from a fairy tale or a medieval joust, beautiful and brightly colored with silk curtains as walls and doors. Together, the three tents formed a reception area with outer and inner court-yards. They were decorated with the colorful flags and banners of the Tokugawa families. It was here that the exchange of the letter would take place.

## The Ceremony Takes Place

At 8:30 A.M., Kayama and Nakajima, dressed in fine silk and velvet suits, came aboard the *Susquehanna*. They would be the official escorts for Perry. At 10:00 A.M., fifteen small boats, loaded with the men of Perry's escort, left the steamship for shore, accompanied by Kayama and Nakajima in their official Japanese boat.

When the boats were halfway to shore, a thunderous salute from thirteen of the *Susquehanna*'s guns signaled the departure of Commodore Perry from his flagship. When the commodore finally stepped onto Japanese soil, it was the first time that any Japanese person had ever seen him. No Japanese had yet spoken directly to him. He was met on the beach by Kayama and Nakajima. They were to escort him to the reception area.

With the American ship's band playing "Hail Columbia" in the background and an escort of officers with drawn swords on each side, Perry marched a few paces ahead of his bodyguards, who carried his pennants and flags. Behind them came two cabin boys.

*An artist's depiction of Perry's troops on parade.*

They carried the rosewood boxes that held President Fillmore's letter and its translations in Dutch and Chinese. No one in Japan could read English, so the letter had to have Dutch and Chinese translations to be sure the Japanese could understand the American letter.

Silently, the Americans followed the two Japanese escorts into the first and largest tent, which served as an outer reception hall and waiting room. Only Perry, the bodyguards, the cabin boys, and several interpreters continued on a red felt pathway into a second, smaller pine structure. Its walls were covered in fine

*A view of the Japanese structures in which the letter exchange ceremony took place.*

purple cloth embroidered with the hollyhocks of the Tokugawa family and paintings of trees and birds.

At the other end of this inner room, Toda Izu and Ido Iwami bowed slightly to the commodore as he entered. Perry was shown to an armchair by Kayama, who acted as the official Japanese interpreter. Neither Japanese ambassador ever spoke a word that morning. In fact, they never looked directly at Perry. Perry, hardened by forty years of naval service and not bothered by their indifference, sat and waited patiently and silently. He had the instincts and patience to know how to make the Japanese respect him.

Soon, the awkward silence was broken by the Japanese declaration that their highnesses were ready to receive the letter. Without speaking, Perry directed the cabin boys to carry the rosewood boxes to a table in front of the Japanese officials. The bodyguards then opened the foot-long boxes. They displayed the letters, with their presidential wax seals encased in six-inch by three-inch solid gold boxes, to the Japanese officials. Then they put the letters back in the rosewood cases.

Ido Iwami then handed his interpreter a scroll, which was handed to one of the Americans. It was an official receipt for the president's letter. The receipt acknowledged that Perry had insisted on delivering the president's letter in Tokyo Bay and that the Japanese had complied. It also said that Japanese law still forbade any communication between Japanese and foreigners, except in Nagasaki. For that reason,

*In this artist's depiction, Commodore Perry delivers President Fillmore's letter to the Japanese.*

the receipt said it would be best for Perry to leave immediately.

Perry thought about this for a few minutes. Then he informed the Japanese officials that he was leaving in a few days for China and would be glad to deliver any messages that the Japanese wanted to send. Again, there was a long silence. Perry then added that he planned to return to Japan in the spring. The Japanese interpreters could not hold their surprise at this news. They asked if he planned to bring all four ships. Probably more, Perry said.

## Source Document

I have directed Commodore Perry to assure your Imperial Majesty that I entertain the kindest feelings towards your Majesty's person and government; and that I have no other object in sending him to Japan, but to propose to your Imperial Majesty that the United States and Japan should live in friendship, and have commercial intercourse with each other. . . .[10]

*An excerpt from the letter President Fillmore sent to Japan with Commodore Perry.*

An even longer silence began. Kayama then informed the Americans that the formal exchange was over. Perry, Toda Izu, and Ido Iwami rose and bowed slightly toward each other. Perry turned and marched out of the room. He was joined by the Americans waiting in the outer reception area. They returned, as they had come, back to the water's edge. With the American military band playing "Yankee Doodle Dandy," Perry boarded his boat and returned to the *Susquehanna*. He was followed by his armed escort of sailors and marines.[11] No fighting had occurred.

Perry was annoyed with the Japanese receipt and its implied order to leave. He decided to show the

*Toda Izu was the negotiator who received President Fillmore's letter.*

Japanese once again that he would do what he wanted, not what they demanded. He ordered the survey boats to continue to map the harbor, moving ever closer to Tokyo itself.

The next day, Perry boarded the *Mississippi* and ordered it to move farther up the bay toward Tokyo. Slowly, the *Mississippi* moved another ten miles north. Then Perry decided that he had gone far enough. He ordered the *Mississippi* to return to its anchorage. Perry decided that his work was done, until the next time.[12]

It appeared that not much had been accomplished. Perry had delivered the letter, but he had received only an order to leave. No Japanese official had even spoken to him. Perry realized, however, what a tremendous advantage he had achieved because of the fear his mighty ships had caused among the Japanese. He had forced the Japanese to break their centuries-old laws prohibiting foreigners and to treat him with respect, if not friendliness. Perry's arrival had also caused a deep division among the ruling Bakufu. In time, this division would lead the Japanese to grant all the requests contained in the president's letter and more. In a letter to his wife, Perry wrote,

> This achievement of mine I consider an important event in my life. The Pageant was magnificent and I am the only Christian that has ever before landed peacefully on this part of Japan or in any part without submitting to the most humiliating degradation. My next visit may prove still more eventful.[13]

At daybreak on July 17, 1853, Perry's Black Fleet left Japanese waters. The *Susquehanna* and the *Mississippi* towed the sailing ships *Saratoga* and *Plymouth* out of the harbor. Crowds of sightseers gathered all along the shore. At least a thousand small boats, filled with Japanese, sailed close to the departing ships to watch them leave. Almost all of them wished the Americans would stay away forever.[14]

After fighting a typhoon off the coast of Japan for several days and stopping briefly in Okinawa to establish trade and a coaling station, the American ships reached Hong Kong on August 17, 1853.[15] Perry planned to overhaul his ships and give his men some much-needed rest and relaxation ashore. Other ships of the United States Navy were scheduled to meet Perry in Hong Kong. With them, he could return to Japan in the spring with a significantly larger and even more threatening fleet.

# Second Trip to Japan, 1854

**W**hile in China, things moved quickly. Perry did not have as much time for repairs and relaxation as he first thought. Once other nations became aware of Perry's actions in Japan, they did not want to be left behind.

Friends in Hong Kong told Perry that the French fleet, also in Hong Kong at the time, was purchasing supplies for an expedition to an unknown destination. Perry guessed that they, too, were going to Japan. The Russian fleet was also in the area. It, too, was rumored to be seeking trade relations with Japan. In fact, on January 3, 1854, Russian Admiral Evfimii Vasilevich Putiatin arrived in Nagasaki with a Russian fleet. The Japanese were just as afraid of Russian cannons as those of the Americans. They promised Putiatin that, if Japan opened trade with any other nation, they would give the same privileges to the Russians.

Putiatin accepted this and withdrew his fleet to await the outcome of Commodore Perry's next visit.

## Perry Returns Early

Perry's fleet had grown to ten ships, including three steamships (the U.S.S. *Powhatan*, the *Mississippi*, and the *Susquehanna*). Perry left Hong Kong on January 14, 1854, with the three steamships. The *Powhatan* and the *Mississippi* each towed a sailing ship. The rest of the American sailing ships had been sent ahead on various missions to China and Okinawa.

Perry arrived in Okinawa on January 21. There, he found the U.S.S. *Vandalia*, U.S.S. *Macedonian*, and U.S.S. *Supply* anchored in the harbor. During the first week of February 1854, Perry sent four sailing ships, the *Lexington*, *Macedonian*, *Southampton*, and *Vandalia*, to Tokyo Bay. Their commander, Captain Joel Abbot, sailed on the *Macedonian*. Meanwhile, Perry continued trade negotiations with the Okinawans. By February 7, Perry had received what he wanted—trade, supplies, and a coaling station. He then left for Japan with the rest of the Black Fleet.[1]

On the morning of February 13, 1854, the American ships slowly went right past Uraga. They stopped well beyond Kannonsaki. Again they anchored, pointing directly into the heart of Tokyo Bay. Perry had returned with more ships and sixteen hundred men. When he arrived just twenty-six miles south of Tokyo, the nightmare began once again for Japanese officials.[2]

*A Japanese official drew this view of one of the ships of Perry's Black Fleet.*

Two Japanese guard boats had followed the American ships from Uraga. As soon as the American ships lowered their anchors, the Japanese came alongside the flagship *Susquehanna* and asked to speak to the commodore. Perry, ill in his cabin, would again leave all contact with the Japanese to his subordinates. The Japanese were directed to Captain Henry Adams on the *Powhatan*.

Adams informed the Japanese, after their usual protests, that the Americans would remain where they were and would not return to Uraga. If the Japanese were unhappy with that, the Americans could move closer to Tokyo.[3] No, replied the Japanese, the American ships could stay where they were.

The pattern established in 1853 continued in 1854. The Americans did what they wanted, the Japanese protested, the Americans threatened to move closer to Tokyo, and the Japanese gave in. The tactic had worked during the Americans' last visit and it succeeded again in 1854. The Japanese were helpless against the technological might of the Americans. Still, the Japanese were certainly not going to admit their weakness or give up.

When negotiations with the new Japanese officials quickly broke down about where formal discussions about the content of President Fillmore's letter—the letter Perry had delivered the previous year—would take place, Perry moved his fleet. On February 24, 1854, it anchored near the tiny village of Yokohama, only fifteen miles south of Tokyo. American survey boats were sent to within four miles of the Tokyo waterfront. They discovered that the channel was wide and the water at least six fathoms deep. (A fathom is equal to six feet.) These facts meant the American ships would be able to move all the way to the Tokyo waterfront, take positions to fire their cannons on the capital, and turn around when they were done.

## The Japanese Response

The American approach to Tokyo had the effect Perry had hoped for. Kayama came to the flagship and told Captain Adams that the Americans could choose a suitable area ashore for the site of the new negotiations.[4] Over the winter, the Bakufu had decided to give in to the American demands. Although negotiations between the two sides were still difficult, both understood that the final outcome had already been decided. There was less tension than before. That did not mean there were no more threats or delays. Superiors in the Bakufu told Japanese officials to try to delay the opening of the ports for five years. If that did not work, they should delay for three years. They were told to tell the Americans that they could be provided with coal, but only on the island of Kyushu. They could get other supplies only at Nagasaki.

On March 3, Perry told Kayama that the United States was prepared to go to war to get what it wanted. Kayama kept trying to find out the absolute minimum that the Americans would settle for. Back and forth, back and forth, the negotiations were slow going.

Formal negotiations were scheduled to begin on land on March 8. On that day, Perry went ashore with an escort of five hundred fully armed men and three bands. The bands played "The Star-Spangled Banner" as he stepped off his boat. He was met inside the reception hall by fifty-five-year-old Hayashi Daigaku who was the *no kami*, or top official, of the University of Tokyo. He had been appointed by the Bakufu as the chief negotiator. With Hayashi were five other official negotiators.

## Terms of the Treaty

The Japanese quickly offered the Americans several concessions. They promised to aid distressed ships with coal, wood, water, and provisions. They would return stranded sailors. They would also prepare a harbor within five years that would supply coal to American ships. However, nothing was mentioned about trade.

Perry replied that the Japanese offers were good, but asked about a trade agreement between Japan and the United States. Hayashi replied that Japan was self-sufficient. It did not want trade with any foreign governments, other than the Dutch and the Chinese. Perry pointed out that both Japan and the United States would prosper through a trade agreement. The United States wanted a trade treaty similar to the one it had with China, the Treaty of Wanghia. Perry gave

Hayashi a copy of that treaty. Perry added that he was prepared to remain in Tokyo Bay until he received favorable responses to all his requests.

The talks ended in the evening without any final decisions about trade. Perry noted that night, however, that the Japanese were willing to give him more than he had thought they would. Still, he decided he would continue to press for more.[5]

It soon became apparent that the Americans were about to get what they wanted. With this realization, the mood relaxed and changed to one of curious cooperation.

## Presents

On the morning of March 13, 1854, Captain Henry Adams of the *Powhatan* went ashore with Jesse Gay, the chief engineer of the *Mississippi*, and a crew of sailors. They were to set up the presents that Commodore Perry had brought from the United States for the emperor of Japan and his high officials. As the numerous crates were unpacked, the Japanese were astonished at the beauty and novelty of items they had never seen before.

The most incredible gift was a miniature steam railroad, complete with a locomotive, a tender (the car that carries a locomotive's fuel and water), and a passenger car. The train rode on an eighteen-inch-gauge track that was built in a circle, three hundred fifty feet in diameter. The engineer had to sit on the tender in order to operate the locomotive. The coach, too small

## Source Document

Meanwhile the implements of husbandry had been put together and exhibited, the track laid down, and the beautiful little engine with its tiny car set in motion. It could be seen from the ship, flying round its circular path exciting the utmost wonder in the minds of the Japanese. Although this perfect piece of machinery was with its car finished in the most tasteful manner, it was much smaller than I had expected it would have been, the car being incapable of admitting with any comfort even a child of six years. The Japanese therefore who rode upon it were seated upon the roof, whilst the engineer placed himself upon the tender.[6]

*Commodore Perry described how he and his crew introduced the Japanese to many new technologies previously unavailable in Japan, including a miniature steam-operated train.*

to hold a six-year-old child, was beautifully paneled in several shades of rosewood. Once the train was put into operation, many of the Japanese took a ride by sitting on top of the coach car, their robes flying behind them as the train huffed, puffed, and whistled around the track.

Another technologically advanced present was a telegraph. The American engineers set up two battery-run telegraph stations and strung wire on telegraph poles between them. The device completely mystified the Japanese, who knew nothing of electricity. No matter how fast they ran between the two stations, the telegraph operator at one station already knew the message they brought from the other station.

The Americans also brought a folding ladder and a long-handled pruning saw, which were very popular. Other gifts included a mechanical water pump with a long hose to attach to it. The Japanese officials found the water hose great fun and soon turned the spray on the two to three hundred spectators. One of the American engineers put one of the folding ladders against the wall of a nearby house, took the hose, climbed to the top, and sprayed the roof to show the Japanese a better way to fight the fires that endangered their neighborhoods, which were filled with wooden buildings.

Among many other gifts the Americans brought books, maps, tools, photographs, whiskey, champagne, and eight boxes of Irish potatoes. Of all the presents, however, the most popular were the guns—the six-shot

Colt revolvers and the twenty-four-shot Hays rifles. This was the part of the technological revolution that the militant Japanese respected most. They all wanted to see the firepower of the new deadly weapons.[7]

These presents had been chosen by Perry and paid for out of his own pocket to make an impression on the Japanese about the vast superiority of American technology. The Japanese remained convinced that they were the most civilized and cultured people of all the world. However, Perry's gifts made them realize that they were far behind the Americans and Europeans in military technology. The Americans might be barbarians, but they were very powerful barbarians.

At the same time, the Japanese began to send much-needed supplies to the American ships. Eggs, chickens, ducks, fish, wheat, rice, sweet potatoes, and green vegetables were loaded on barges and delivered to the fleet. The food was especially appreciated by the sailors. They had been living on salt pork and hard biscuits aboard ship.[8]

## What Was Trade and What Was Help?

On March 17, 1854, Perry met with Hayashi once more. Again, he brought up the subject of trade between the two countries. Perry asked Hayashi if the Japanese were ready to supply provisions to ships that went to Japan for help but were not in distress. Hayashi replied that the Japanese would not sell provisions to American ships. Perry responded that

American ships in distress would like to pay for the supplies they received. Hayashi replied that no payment was necessary; the provisions were gifts. Perry inquired whether the Americans could give gifts in return for the supplies. Hayashi responded that, if they were gifts, the Japanese could receive them. Perry wondered if the Japanese would prefer gifts of manufactured goods or gold and silver. Hayashi responded that gold and silver would be fine. Under the guise of discussing gifts, Perry and the Japanese had set up a system for future trade.

Next, Perry told Hayashi that Nagasaki was not an acceptable port for American ships to visit. He wanted the Japanese to open other ports, maybe five or six of them, for American ships to use. The Japanese finally agreed that the Americans could use the port of Shimoda. Hayashi also said the Bakufu might decide on another port to open in the next week or so. Hayashi returned to Tokyo to report that he had given in to the further demands of the foreigner. He left it up to the Bakufu to decide which other Japanese port would be opened to American ships.

Perry immediately sent the *Vandalia* and the *Southampton* to Shimoda to report on the suitability of the harbor. He also sent the *Susquehanna* to China on other business. The mood was now one of celebration, although there were still a powerful few of the Bakufu who advocated a suicide attack on the "foreign devils," as the Japanese called the Americans. They remained the minority, however. The Bakufu soon sent word to

Perry that Hakodate, a beautiful port in northern Japan, would also be opened to the ships of the United States.

## Japanese Gifts

On March 24, 1854, Perry received gifts from the Japanese officials. The Japanese presented Perry and his officers with beautifully wrapped boxes, stacked in piles, and arranged by the rank of the recipient. Perry's stack was the biggest. The boxes contained silks and other embroidered cloths, delicate porcelain cups and saucers, writing tablets, fans, coral, and paper. In a private ceremony, Perry was also given two sets of Japanese gold and silver coins, three matchlock guns, and two samurai swords. As a special present from the emperor to the president of the United States, the Japanese gave the Americans four small dogs. They so resembled King Charles spaniels that Perry believed the English breed had descended from a pair like these that had been sent to King Charles of England by the emperor of Japan in 1612.[9]

After the presentation of gifts, the Japanese invited the Americans to witness a demonstration of sumo, the Japanese form of wrestling. Some thirty sumo wrestlers paraded before the Americans and proved their strength by carrying several one-hundred-fifty-pound bags of rice at a time to the American barges at the water's edge. Some carried the bags in their teeth. The wrestlers then staged a series of bouts that lasted only a few seconds each. The huge men rushed at one another. With one blow or sidestep, the winner caused the loser to fall out or be thrown from the tiny circular ring. The Americans found these bloodless matches very different from the bloody, bare-knuckled boxing matches they watched at home, which often lasted for several hours.

The Americans then staged a demonstration of military drill. This show of military discipline greatly pleased the Japanese. Three days later, Perry entertained the Japanese officials aboard the *Powhatan*. Perry dined with the five highest-ranking Japanese officials in his stateroom. Outside, sixty other officials feasted on beef, mutton, game, poultry, and fish. After dinner, the band played, the ship's crew put on entertainment, and toast after toast was drunk with wine, sweetened whiskey, and champagne. When all the intoxicating spirits were gone, a mixture of tomato ketchup and vinegar was served. The Japanese seemed to like it just fine. When the Japanese officials, most of them drunk, were leaving the ship, one of them threw his arm around Perry's shoulders. He leaned his head on Perry's arm and repeated over and over, "Nippon [Japan] and America, all the same heart." When one of the American officers tried to make him move along, Perry replied, "Oh, if he will only sign the treaty, he may kiss me."[10]

## Treaty of Kanagawa

Finally, on March 31, 1854, the negotiations came to an end. The Americans wrote their version of the agreement in Dutch, Chinese, and English. The Japanese composed their version in Dutch, Chinese, and Japanese. The two sides met ashore and compared the documents written in Dutch and Chinese. When they agreed that the two documents were the same, they signed them. Because Yokohama, where the treaty was signed, was in the district of Kanagawa, the treaty became known as the Treaty of Kanagawa.

Once the formalities were over, Perry was very happy. Although he was generally stern in nature, he was gracious in speech and manner. He had not known about the strict laws of Japan when he arrived, he said. He offered guns and warships if the Japanese needed them. He said he only wanted the two countries to be friends and to prosper together.

The treaty opened the port of Shimoda to American ships immediately. The port of Hakodate would be opened in one year. Under the treaty, no other ports were to be used by American shipping, except in an emergency. Shipwrecked sailors were to be taken to either of the American ports, to be returned to the United States. An American diplomat would be welcomed at Shimoda eighteen months after the signing of the treaty. The United States would automatically receive whatever privileges Japan later granted to any other nation. The only thing that Perry did not get that he really wanted was a commercial trade agreement. But that would come later, he believed. On April 4, 1854, the *Saratoga* sailed for the United States with the treaty.[11]

For the next three months, Perry remained in Japanese waters. He visited the ports of Shimoda and Hakodate. Both ports were spacious and secure. Perry stayed long enough in each place to be sure that the spirit as well as the letter of the treaty was being observed by the Japanese.

On June 25, 1854, Commodore Perry, aboard the *Powhatan*, with the *Southampton* in tow, steamed out of Shimoda Harbor toward Hong Kong.[12] Perry had requested that he be allowed to leave the fleet at Hong Kong so that he could return to the United States. He considered his mission accomplished. He was tired. The constant humidity and the harsh life of sea duty had made his arthritis worse. He wanted to go home.

## Chapter 6

# Perry at Home

$O$nce the mission to Japan was over, Matthew Perry was anxious to return to his family. He was perfectly content to leave the fleet in Hong Kong to find its own way back to the United States. Perry wanted to travel as light as possible. It would take him ten weeks to reach Europe, using two different steamship lines and four or five different railroads to get there. All of Perry's notes and papers from the expedition were left aboard the *Mississippi*. All the gifts he received from the Japanese, as well as some three hundred living trees, plants, and shrubs he was bringing to the United States, were stored aboard the *Plymouth* and the *Lexington*.

## The Trip Home

Perry, Lieutenant Silas Bent, and an orderly left Hong Kong aboard the British steamer H.M.S. *Hindostan* on

September 11, 1854. As he left the fleet for the last time, the men of the *Mississippi* sent Perry a message: "We shall never feel greater confidence, or stronger pride, than while under your command."[1]

From Suez, at the entrance to the Red Sea, Perry and his party took a train to Cairo, another to Alexandria, and finally, a steamship to Trieste. Once the trip was under way, Perry's good spirits and health seemed to return. He knew he was approaching his loved ones at home.

News of Perry's success in Japan preceded him. At the time, there were no telephone or telegraph lines to link Asia to Europe or the United States. No immediate communication was possible. During Perry's stays in Japan, he could neither relay information to the United States government nor receive orders. He was on his own. Perry's success was considered so important that news of it was sent in the mail of foreign diplomats, which was carried to their home countries in Europe by the fastest ships available.

In Trieste, Archduke Charles of Austria, the brother of Emperor Franz Joseph of the Austro-Hungarian Empire, invited Perry to an intimate family dinner. The archduke wanted to learn about the mysterious land of Japan. Perry traveled by train to Vienna, through Germany, and on to The Hague, the capital of the Netherlands. At each of his stops, royal and political figures offered him dinners and praise for his success. Everyone was eager to learn about the Japanese.

At The Hague, Perry stayed with August Belmont, the current American minister to the Netherlands, who was married to Perry's daughter Caroline. She wrote in her diary on November 20, 1854, "Papa has arrived, in good health & spirits, he is looking uncommonly well, & seems delighted to get once more among us."[2] The family enjoyed a happy reunion with lavish dinners and early Christmas parties. The king and queen of the Netherlands formally received Perry at a small ceremony. They, too, were eager to hear the news of Japan.[3]

But Perry was soon back at work. On December 7, 1854, he left for England to inspect some new British steamships. He wanted to see if they had any improvements worth copying in the design of six new war steamers the United States Navy planned to build.

Perry also talked to noted author Nathaniel Hawthorne, who was working as the American consul at Liverpool. He wanted Hawthorne to write the official story of Perry's expedition to Japan. Hawthorne turned him down, but said it would certainly be an interesting topic to write about.

## Results of the Expedition

Perry left Liverpool aboard the H.M.S. *Baltic*, a British steamer, on December 30. He arrived in New York on January 11, 1855. There was little comment from the United States government when Perry returned. The *Mississippi*, carrying all of Perry's papers, continued west to east around the world, finally arriving in New

*A Japanese artist drew this image of cargo being loaded onto an American ship after trade opened with Japan.*

York in April 1855. It became the first steamship to circumnavigate the globe. Perry met the ship when it docked.

Perry never received much official recognition from the United States government for the expedition. Times had changed since he had left for Japan. The United States that, in 1850, was ready to spread American influence and democracy to the farthest corners of the globe, was, by 1855, more concerned with problems at home. Fights over slavery and states' rights were the consuming passions of the country. There was armed conflict in Kansas between pro- and antislavery factions. The western territories that the United States had won in the Mexican War had caused violent conflict over whether Congress or the states had the right to determine whether slavery should exist in American territories. At this point, westward and global expansion were ideas that had only caused problems at home. Hatred was in the air, and public opinion in the United States did not care much about whether the Japanese on the other side of the world wanted American trade.

In the midst of the political fights, Perry bought a brick house at 38 West Thirty-second Street in New York City and filled it with furniture he had shipped from Hong Kong. The American government may no longer have been interested in trade with Japan, but the bankers of New York were. The Perry family was accepted into New York high society, and the commodore often accompanied his daughter Isabella to fancy dances and dinners around town.[4] He was soundly applauded by the businessmen of New York and New England. He was honored with dinners and ceremonies, often accompanied by expensive presents.

## Publishing an Account of the Expedition

Perry continued to serve in the navy, but he was given only a few assignments that kept him in the New York area. Perry devoted most of his time to seeing that a good record of his achievements in Japan was published.

Perry persuaded Francis Hawks, the rector of Calvary Church in New York, to edit what he saw as a readable and popular account of the scientific, cultural, and diplomatic accomplishments of the expedition. The two men rented rooms at the American Bible Society's office and got to work.

The first volume was ready for the printers after only seven months of work. The second and third volumes appeared in 1857.[5] The book was called the *Narrative of the Expedition of an American Squadron to the China Seas and Japan*. Volume one was a narrative account of the expedition. It was beautifully and expensively illustrated with full-color plates and lithographs by William Heine and other artists who had accompanied the expedition. It contained a study of Japanese, Okinawan, and Chinese society, as well as a history of the expedition itself.

The United States government paid about $400,000 to print 34,000 copies of the three volumes. Over half of these were given to members of Congress, and two thousand were given to the Navy Department. Perry received a thousand copies. He gave half of these to his editor, Francis Hawks.

The first volume came out in April 1856. The printer thought it was such a desirable book that he printed an extra fifteen hundred copies for himself. Although Congress promised to pay for the books, it gave Perry no money to write them. Soon he could not afford to pay Hawks to help him. He was forced to complete the editing of volumes two and three by himself.[6]

Volume two was a collection of scientific essays written by members of the expedition. It included articles on the geology of Okinawa, coal deposits on the island of Formosa, the botany of Okinawa, and a survey of the west coast of Japan. In addition, there were studies of topics such as cyclones, birds, and shells.

Plants had been collected by the ship's doctors, scientists, and a Chinese gardener during the expedition. They were all put on board the *Lexington* for the trip back to the United States. The more than three hundred living species were kept outside on the deck of the ship. The crew built a cover above the plants to protect them from the salt spray of the ocean and the hot tropical sun.

When the *Lexington* reached the Brooklyn Navy Yard on February 16, 1855, most of the plants were still alive. They were transported to Washington, D.C., where they were placed in several greenhouses Congress had built for them on the Capitol grounds. Dried specimens were taken to Harvard College to be classified by Dr. Asa Gray, the most important biologist of the day. Gray and his co-workers examined and classified the plants and returned a list to Perry just in time to include it as a chapter in volume two of the *Narrative*. Unfortunately, a Japanese vocabulary, also planned for the volume, was never finished. Volume three was a study of zodiacal light, an astronomical and navigational science that is no longer popularly known.

## Death of the Commodore

In February 1858, two months after the publication of the last part of the *Narrative*, Matthew Perry, now almost sixty-four years old, caught a cold. It was a bitterly cold winter, and the illness persisted and grew worse. It was complicated by Perry's arthritis. Perry grew weaker and became unable to climb the stairs to his bedroom. His family made a makeshift bedroom out of the library downstairs at their home and moved Perry into it. At 2:00 A.M. on March 5, 1858, Commodore Perry died.

For three days, flags on public buildings and ships flew at half-mast. The funeral parade on Saturday, March 6, 1858, was a public event sponsored by the New York City government. The men who marched beside the casket included heroes of the Mexican War.

*This portrait of Matthew Perry, the man who opened Japan to trade, was done in 1854.*

Behind the casket marched a uniformed group of fifty officers and men who had served with the commodore in the Japanese expedition. Behind them marched several hundred men from the 7th Regiment and two hundred officers from the 1st Division of the New York state militia.

The streets were crowded with onlookers, despite the bitterly cold weather, as the funeral procession marched along the streets of downtown Manhattan. The procession marched from Perry's house on Thirty-second Street to St. Mark's Church on Tenth Street. The bells in the church steeple rang, and every minute during the funeral service, a cannon was fired in salute from one of the United States Navy ships in the nearby harbor.

After the service, Commodore Perry's casket was placed in the Slidell family vault next to the casket of his daughter, Anna, who had died in infancy. Marines fired a final salute of three volleys over the vault. The funeral was over.

# Chapter 7

# Japan After Perry

Although the United States quickly turned its attention away from the Pacific Ocean, for the Japanese, Commodore Perry's visit was an event that changed their country forever. In 1858, Townsend Harris, the new American ambassador at Shimoda, completed the formal trade agreement with the Japanese government that had been agreed upon during Perry's negotiations.

Japanese leaders were immediately confronted with demands from other world powers for the same privileges. The Dutch, who were still bound by the centuries-old trade agreement that limited them to one visit a year at only one port, petitioned to be allowed the same trading privileges as the Americans. The Russians then arrived at Nagasaki, followed by the British and the French. In all, the fleets of seventeen other nations arrived over the next several years,

# Source Document

... I addressed the Tai-kun as follows: "May it please your Majesty: In presenting my letters of credence from the President of the United States, I am directed to express to your Majesty the sincere wishes of the President for your health and happiness and for the prosperity of your dominions. I consider it a great honor that I have been selected to fill the high and important place of Plenipotentiary of the United States at the court of your Majesty, and as my earnest wishes are to unite the two countries more closely in the ties of enduring friendship, my constant exertions shall be directed to the attainment of that happy end."[1]

*Townsend Harris was the first United States ambassador to Japan after Commodore Perry's successful expedition. He described his experience in meeting the Japanese.*

seeking trade agreements. The Japanese were forced to accept each of the European nations as a trading partner under terms they felt were unfair.[2]

The foreign invasion left the Japanese feeling hopeless. They waited for the day that their country could become strong enough to throw off its foreign obligations. To most Japanese leaders and soldiers, this was humiliating. The two hundred years of peace and security that isolation had brought them were gone. Most of the Japanese people began to hate foreigners more than before. Most felt that their leaders had let them down and could no longer rule.[3]

In southern Japan, the Satsuma family began to build its own navy. In Choshu province in western Japan, new army regiments were created, using peasants as soldiers. The shogun and the Bakufu were losing control of the country.

## Restoration of the Emperor

The emperor had been isolated in his castle in Kyoto during Perry's visits. He had not even been told of Perry's visit. He had not been responsible for the nation's humiliation. Many young samurai turned to the teenage emperor, Mutsuhito, as the symbol of their desire for change. They began to look to the emperor, instead of the shogun, for new leadership. Divided loyalties grew among the people until a civil war broke out.

In January 1868, the forces of the Tokugawa family were defeated in a battle with army regiments under the control of the unhappy young samurai officers. A new government was proclaimed in the name of the emperor, who changed his name to Meiji, which means "Enlightened Rule."[4] The next year, the emperor moved his capital to Tokyo from Kyoto. He began to pass new laws that formally ended isolation and made Japan a modern industrialized nation.

At first, no one knew exactly what form of government would suit Japan. More than twenty forms were tried. In spite of this uncertain beginning, between 1871 and 1875, the new government made several important changes. It created a national land tax. Peasants were given titles to their farms but were required to pay taxes in money, not rice, each year. They had to pay the same amount regardless of the rice harvest. From this time on, the majority of the national income came from this land tax. The new government also established a national army using conscription, or the draft. Peasants were called to serve in the army, which now used modern weapons and tactics. The military was no longer the exclusive domain of the samurai class.

In 1876, the new government outlawed the wearing of samurai swords in public. It did this to destroy the powerful public image of the old samurai warriors. The next year, the old warriors rebelled in what is called the Satsuma Rebellion. They were soundly defeated by the new conscription army. The laws that maintained the four social classes in Japanese society were also abolished. The Japanese people quickly adopted Western-style clothing and manners.

The national government gave financial support to begin building steel and cement plants. Factories of all kinds were established. Roads, harbors, and telegraphs were constructed and improved. Most of all, the attitude of the people changed. A new Japanese patriotism prospered. People worked hard to make Japan equal to any other world power. To do this, they adopted Western technology and the educational system that was needed to have a technological economy. In just a few years, these changes marked the end of divided regional political power and the beginning of a truly national government in Japan.

## Foreign Expansion

The Japanese have characteristically valued hard work and attention to detail. Before long, the Meiji Restoration, as this period in Japanese history has come to be called, produced a powerful, modern nation. Japan soon turned its attention to its relations with foreign powers.

In 1893, the Korean king requested the ruler of China to send troops to aid him in putting down a rebellion. A treaty between China and Japan at that time required either side to inform the other if they moved army units into Korea. When the Chinese informed the Japanese that they planned to send troops in support of the Korean king, Japan decided to send an equal number of troops. Both sides prepared for war against each other, as they did often, with the Koreans as their common victims.

In August 1893, Japanese troops stormed the national palace in Seoul, the capital of Korea, and captured the king. The Japanese defeated the Chinese Army and Navy in nearly every battle they fought. Within months, the Chinese asked for peace.

The Japanese demanded that China pay a fine and the war costs, as well as give Korea its independence and cede the Chinese territories of Manchuria and Formosa to Japan. The Chinese agreed, but Russia, Germany, and France told Japan that it could not have Manchuria. Instead, the Japanese could increase the fine. At this time, the Western powers of Europe continued to consider China and Japan weak nations. The Europeans were determined to impose their desires on the Asian nations. It was the same attitude of superiority that Perry had used to impose his will thirty years before. The Japanese felt humiliated by this continual interference by the Western powers, but agreed to their demands for the same reason that they had agreed to Perry's demands in the first place—fear of the West's military superiority.

The Japanese waited ten more years to take their revenge on Russia for interfering in Manchuria. In those ten years, Japan continued to modernize and build more heavy industries, roads, electric power plants, and a better and stronger army and navy. Russia continued to expand its influence into northern China and Korea. By this time, England was just as interested as Japan in limiting Russian influence in the Pacific Ocean region. In 1902, England and Japan signed a treaty of friendship. It ensured that no other Western nation would help Russia in the event of a Russian-Japanese war. It was just the opening that Japan had long awaited.

On February 8, 1904, the Japanese Navy struck suddenly and sank much of the Russian fleet while it was in the Pacific coast harbor of Port Arthur. Then Japan formally declared war on Russia. Most of the world thought that Russia would easily defeat the Japanese, but world opinion underestimated the Japanese. The well-trained and dedicated Japanese Army won nearly every battle, even in the frozen winters of the Manchurian wilderness. It was a costly war. More than seventy thousand Japanese soldiers were killed at the Battle of Mukden alone. Within months, the Russians were seeking peace.[5]

The war ended with the Treaty of Portsmouth, arranged by Theodore Roosevelt, the president of the United States. The Japanese were forced to take less than they felt they were due. They received territories in Manchuria and Korea, but the Russians were not forced to repay Japan for the money it had borrowed from England and the United States to pay for the war. Again, the Japanese felt humiliated by the inter-ference of Western countries in the peace terms of victories won at a price of many Japanese lives.[6]

# Japan as a World Power

In 1912, Emperor Meiji died after forty-five years of rule. His grandson, Hirohito, became the regent for his father, the sickly Emperor Taisho. Taisho died in 1926. Hirohito then became the new emperor.

At that time, Japan was one of the most accomplished nations on earth. It was a democracy where all adult males could vote. It had a well-educated, prosperous middle class of factory workers.

Japan continued to expand its influence around the world. During the 1930s, Japan conducted another brutal war against China to win Manchuria, with its mineral and oil deposits. This time, Japan refused to obey the Western powers' orders to stop. But this time, the Western powers had no time to worry about Japan. They were involved in a war in Europe.

When Nazi Germany attacked Poland in 1939 to begin World War II in Europe, Japan saw an opportunity to finally take revenge on the United States and the Western powers. Japan, therefore, allied itself with Germany and Italy against the Allies—Great Britain, France, the Soviet Union, and eventually, the United States. On December 7, 1941, a Japanese attack force struck Pearl Harbor, Hawaii, in an attempt to destroy the American naval fleet stationed there.

After years of brutal fighting both in Europe and in the Pacific, the Allies would win World War II. The Japanese, however, proved themselves a valiant enemy. Even after Germany and Italy had surrendered, Japan continued its fight against the Allies. It

## Source Document

We hereby proclaim the unconditional surrender to the Allied Powers of the Japanese Imperial General Headquarters and of all Japanese armed forces and all armed forces under the Japanese control wherever situated.

We hereby command all Japanese forces wherever situated and the Japanese people to cease hostilities forthwith . . . and to comply with all requirements which may be imposed by the Supreme Commander for the Allied Powers or by agencies of the Japanese Government at his direction.[7]

*After the bombing of Hiroshima and Nagasaki, the Japanese finally surrendered to Allied forces, bringing World War II to an end.*

would take the United States' use of a new, horrible weapon—the atomic bomb—to force the Japanese to surrender at last, in September 1945.

Finally, the tensions that had become war were over. Japan and the United States would once again have to make agreements for the rebuilding of the postwar world.

# Chapter 8

# Defeat and National Rebirth

At daybreak on September 2, 1945, the Japanese Army chief of staff, the foreign minister, and a delegation of other officials left the destroyed ruins of Tokyo, still smoking from bombs and fires. They traveled to Yokohama to board the U.S.S. *Missouri*, the American flagship anchored in the same place that Matthew Perry had used to conclude the Treaty of Kanagawa nearly a hundred years before.

Everything that the Japanese had feared when Perry first appeared in Japan had come true. Japan had finally been defeated by the technological superiority of another nation. The cities of Japan were destroyed. Hundreds of thousands of Japanese civilians were dead. Many suffered from radiation poisoning that would eat away their bodies, the result of the two atomic bombs that had been dropped on Hiroshima and Nagasaki.

General Douglas MacArthur, the commander of the American fleet in Tokyo Bay, accepted the Japanese surrender. He later addressed an American radio audience, saying,

> We stand in Tokyo today reminiscent of our countryman, Commodore Perry, ninety-two years ago. His purpose was to bring to Japan an era of enlightenment and progress, by lifting the veil of isolation to the friendship, trade, and commerce of the world. But alas the knowledge thereby gained of Western science was forged into an instrument of oppression and human enslavement.[1]

After World War II ended, Japan adopted a new constitution that no longer allowed the use of military force except for national defense. Since then, Japan has turned its attention once again to becoming a respected world economic power. The Japanese have become leaders in the automotive and electronics industries. The country has become prosperous once again, is a democratic partner of the United States, and acts as an advocate for nuclear disarmament.

Today, few people in either Japan or the United States even know who Matthew Perry was or the incredible consequences that his desire to open trade between the two countries brought into the world. The United States quickly lost interest in Japan after Perry's success, and Matthew Calbraith Perry remains a relatively minor figure in American history. His visit to Japan, however, introduced huge changes in that country's history. Perry's memory is more alive in Japan's national life than in that of the United States.

# Source Document

**Article 9:**

Aspiring sincerely to an international peace based on justice and order, the Japanese people forever renounce war as a sovereign right of the nation and the threat or use of force as means of settling international disputes. . . .

In order to accomplish the aim of the preceding paragraph, land, sea, and air forces, as well as other war potential, will never be maintained. The right of belligerency of the state will not be recognized.[2]

*After World War II, Japan adopted a new constitution, which renounced war as a means of settling problems.*

In 1901, on the site of the reception hall at Kurihama, a granite shaft was erected in memory of the commodore's visit. It was unveiled by Rear Admiral Frederick Rodgers, a great-nephew of Commodore Perry, and a memorial address was read by Japanese Premier Viscount Katsura. The monument was knocked down by Japanese patriots in 1944, but it was restored during a celebration of the one-hundredth anniversary of Perry's visit in 1953. Today, despite the reluctance and fear the Japanese felt at Perry's first arrival, there are Black Fleet festivals held at the ports of Shimoda, Hakodate, and Naha each year, demonstrating that the Japanese regard Perry, in some ways, as a positive figure in their national history.[3]

**Timeline**

**1794**—*April 10*: Matthew Calbraith Perry born at Newport, Rhode Island.

**1809**—*January 16*: Perry joins the United States Navy as a midshipman.

**1811**—*May 16*: Perry sees his first combat aboard U.S.S. *President*.

**1814**—*December 24*: Perry marries Jane Slidell.

**1815**—*July–November*: Perry fights pirates of Algiers aboard U.S.S. *Chippewa*.

**1821**—*July 21*: Perry is given first command, U.S.S. *Shark*, on a mission to Africa.

**1843**—*June 5*: Perry is appointed commodore of Africa squadron.

**1847**—*March 21*: Perry takes command of the United States fleet on east coast of Mexico.

**1852**—*January*: Perry is ordered to take command of forthcoming Japan expedition.

**1853**—*July 8*: The Black Fleet arrives in Tokyo Bay.
*July 14*: Perry delivers President Millard Fillmore's letter to the Japanese at Kurihama.
*July 17*: Perry leaves Japan for Hong Kong, to return the next year.

**1854**—*February 13*: Black Fleet returns to Tokyo Bay.
*March 31*: Treaty of Kanagawa is signed.
*June 25*: Perry and the Black Fleet leave Japan for the last time.
*September 11*: Perry leaves the Black Fleet in Hong Kong and returns home.

**1855**—*January 11*: Perry arrives in New York.

**1857**—*December 28*: Perry completes work on the *Narrative of the Expedition*.

**1858**—*March 4*: Perry dies.

United States Ambassador Townsend Harris completes trade agreement with Japan.

**1868**—*January*: Tokugawa family is ousted from power in Japan and a new government set up under Emperor Meiji.

**1904**—Russo-Japanese War takes place, ending with the Treaty of Portsmouth.

**1912**—Emperor Meiji dies and Taisho becomes emperor.

**1926**—Taisho dies, and Hirohito becomes emperor.

**1931**—Japan begins war with Manchuria.

**1939**—Japan allies with Germany and Italy to fight World War II.

**1941**—Japan attacks Pearl Harbor, Hawaii.

**1945**—United States ends World War II by dropping atomic bombs on the Japanese cities of Hiroshima and Nagasaki.

**1948**—Japan adopts a new constitution that does not allow the use of military force.

Chapter Notes

## Chapter 1. The Black Ships Arrive

1. Louis G. Perez, *The History of Japan* (Westport, Conn.: The Greenwood Press, 1998), p. 83.

2. Edward L. Beach, *The United States Navy* (New York: Henry Holt and Company, 1986), p. 147; Frank M. Bennett, *The Steam Navy of the United States* (Westport, Conn.: The Greenwood Press, 1972), p. 129 ff.

3. Samuel Eliot Morison, *"Old Bruin": Commodore Matthew C. Perry, 1794–1858* (Boston: Little, Brown and Company, 1967), p. 26.

4. Wilhelm Heine, *With Perry in Japan* (Honolulu: University of Hawaii Press, 1990), p. 64.

5. Bennett, pp. 129–130.

6. Peter Booth Wiley, *Yankees in the Land of the Gods* (New York: Viking, 1990), pp. 289–290.

## Chapter 2. Japan

1. Louis G. Perez, *The History of Japan* (Westport, Conn.: The Greenwood Press, 1998), pp. 46–50.

2. Tsuentomo Yamamoto, *Hagakure: The Book of the Samurai*, trans. William S. Wilson (New York: Kodansha International, Ltd., 1979), pp. 17–18.

3. Perez, pp. 50–52.

4. Arthur Walworth, *Black Ships Off Japan: The Story of Commodore Perry's Expedition* (Hamden, Conn.: Archon Books, 1966), p. 5; Perez, pp. 56–57, 61–62.

5. Perez, pp. 61–62.

6. Walworth, p. 7

7. Peter Booth Wiley, *Yankees in the Land of the Gods* (New York: Viking, 1990), p. 31.

8. Walworth, pp. 8–10; Wiley, pp. 32–33.

9. Wiley, pp. 34–35.

10. Ibid., pp. 22–25.

11. Ibid., pp. 26–28; Walworth, pp. 13–14.

12. Samuel Eliot Morison, *"Old Bruin": Commodore Matthew C. Perry, 1794–1858* (Boston: Little, Brown and Company, 1967), p. 266.

13. Wiley, pp. 91–94.

14. Ibid., pp. 96–98.

## Chapter 3. Matthew Perry, the Soul of the United States Navy

1. Peter Booth Wiley, *Yankees in the Land of the Gods* (New York: Viking, 1990), p. 48.

2. Ibid., p. 47.

3. Samuel Eliot Morison, *"Old Bruin": Commodore Matthew C. Perry, 1794–1858* (Boston: Little, Brown and Company, 1967), pp. 62–63.

4. Ibid., pp. 64–66, 68–75.

5. Ibid., pp. 104–115.

6. Ibid., p. 121.

7. Ibid., pp. 128–129, 162.

8. Paul Halsall, "Modern History Sourcebook: The Treaty of Guadaloupe Hidalgo, 2 Feb. 1848," *Modern History Sourcebook*, July 1998, <http://www.fordham.edu/halsall/mod/1848hidalgo.html> (February 16, 2000).

9. Frank M. Bennett, *The Steam Navy of the United States* (Westport, Conn.: The Greenwood Press, 1972), pp. 92–98.

## Chapter 4. Perry's First Visit to the Empire of Japan

1. Peter Booth Wiley, *Yankees in the Land of the Gods* (New York: Viking, 1990), p. 295.

2. Arthur Walworth, *Black Ships Off Japan: The Story of Commodore Perry's Expedition* (Hamden, Conn.: Archon Books, 1966), p. 84; Wiley, p. 293.

3. Wiley, p. 297.

4. Ibid., p. 298.

5. Ibid., p. 301.

6. Ibid., pp. 304–305.

7. David Colbert, ed., "Commodore Perry Opens Japan," *Eyewitness to America: 500 Years of America in the Words of Those Who Saw It Happen* (New York: Pantheon Books, 1997), p. 187.

8. Wiley, pp. 307–308; Walworth, pp. 97–98.

9. Wiley, pp. 312–313.

10. Jackson J. Spielvogel, *World History: The Human Odyssey* (New York: West Educational Publishing, 1998), pp. 786–787.

11. Samuel Eliot Morison, *"Old Bruin": Commodore Matthew C. Perry, 1794–1858* (Boston: Little, Brown and Company, 1967), pp. 331–335; Wiley, pp. 316–321; Walworth, pp. 100–102.

12. Wiley, pp. 323–324.

13. Morison, p. 335.

14. Wiley, p. 325.

15. Ibid., pp. 348, 353–354.

## Chapter 5. Second Trip to Japan, 1854

1. Peter Booth Wiley, *Yankees in the Land of the Gods* (New York: Viking, 1990), pp. 377–381.

2. Ibid., p. 386.

3. Ibid., p. 387.

4. Ibid., p. 395.

5. Ibid., p. 404.

6. Commodore Matthew C. Perry, "The Japanese Are Introduced to Western Technology, March 1854," *Eyewitness to History*, ed. John Carey (New York: Avon Books, 1997), p. 333.

7. Samuel Eliot Morison, *"Old Bruin": Commodore Matthew C. Perry, 1794–1858* (Boston: Little, Brown and Company, 1967), pp. 371–372; Arthur Walworth, *Black Ships Off Japan: The Story of Commodore Perry's Expedition* (Hamden, Conn.: Archon Books, 1966), pp. 194–196; Wilhelm Heine, *With Perry in Japan* (Honolulu: University of Hawaii Press, 1990), pp. 126–127.

8. Wiley, p. 409.

9. Morison, p. 373; Walworth, pp. 197–198.

10. Morison, pp. 373, 377–378; Wiley, p. 418.

11. Wiley, p. 420.

12. Walworth, pp. 218–222.

## Chapter 6. Perry at Home

1. Arthur Walworth, *Black Ships Off Japan: The Story of Commodore Perry's Expedition* (Hamden, Conn.: Archon Books, 1966), p. 228.

2. Samuel Eliot Morison, *"Old Bruin": Commodore Matthew C. Perry, 1794–1858* (Boston: Little, Brown and Company, 1967), p. 412.

3. Ibid.

4. Ibid., p. 418.

5. Ibid., p. 430.

6. Peter Booth Wiley, *Yankees in the Land of the God*s (New York: Viking, 1990), pp. 463–464.

## Chapter 7. Japan After Perry

1. Paul Halsall, "Modern History Sourcebook: Townsend Harris: The President's Letter," *Modern History Sourcebook*, August 1998, <http://www.fordham.edu/halsall.mod/harris-japan.html> (February 16, 2000).

2. Wilhelm Heine, *With Perry in Japan* (Honolulu: University of Hawaii Press, 1990), pp. 234–235.

3. Louis G. Perez, *The History of Japan* (Westport, Conn.: The Greenwood Press, 1998), p. 86.

4. Ibid., p. 91.

5. Ibid., pp. 122–123.

6. Ibid., p. 124.

7. The University of Oklahoma Law Center, "The Japanese Surrender Documents of World War II," *Chronology of U.S. Historical Documents*, n.d., <http://www.law.ou.edu/hist/japsurr.html> (February 16, 2000).

## Chapter 8. Defeat and National Rebirth

1. Peter Booth Wiley, *Yankees in the Land of the Gods* (New York: Viking, 1990), p. 485.

2. Paul Halsall, "Modern History Sourcebook: The Constitution of Japan, 1946," *Modern History Sourcebook*, August 1997, <http://www.fordham.edu/halsall/mod/CONST-JP.html> (February 16, 2000).

3. Samuel Eliot Morison, *"Old Bruin": Commodore Matthew C. Perry, 1794–1858* (Boston: Little, Brown and Company, 1967), p. 442.

## Further Reading

### Books

Heine, Wilhelm. *With Perry to Japan*. Honolulu: University of Hawaii Press, 1990.

*Japan*. New York: Time-Life Books, 1985.

Perez, Louis G. *The History of Japan*. Westport, Conn.: The Greenwood Press, 1998.

Wiley, Peter Booth. *Yankees in the Land of the Gods*. New York: Viking, 1990.

### Internet Addresses

Beinecke Rare Book & Manuscript Library, Yale University. "The Opening of Japan to the West." *Beinecke Library Home Page*. 1997.
<http://www.library.yale.edu/beinecke/orient/japan.htm> (April 19, 2000).

*Edo World*. n.d.
<http://j-entertain.co.jp/Bellsystem/SharakuWorld/Edoinformation/Edohome.html> (April 19, 2000).

McGee, Mark. *A Brief History of the Samurai*. March 5, 2000. <http://www.mindspring.com/~mamcgee/iaido_samurai.html> (April 19, 2000).

*National Archives of Japan*. n.d.
<http://www.soritu/go/jp/Koubunsho/index_e.html> (April 19, 2000).

# Index